MW00583737

That Famous Fig Leaf

That Famous Fig Leaf

Uncovering the Holiness of Our Bodies

Chad W. Thompson

CASCADE *Books* • Eugene, Oregon

THAT FAMOUS FIG LEAF
Uncovering the Holiness of Our Bodies

Cascade Books
An Imprint of Wipf and Stock Publishers
199 W. 8th Ave., Suite 3
Eugene, OR 97401

www.wipfandstock.com

PAPERBACK ISBN: 978-1-5326-5986-7
HARDCOVER ISBN: 978-1-5326-5987-4
EBOOK ISBN: 978-1-5326-5988-1

Cataloguing-in-Publication data:

Names: Thompson, Chad W., author.

Title: That famous fig leaf : uncovering the holiness of our bodies / by Chad W. Thompson.

Description: Eugene, OR: Cascade Books, 2019 | Includes bibliographical references.

Identifiers: ISBN 978-1-5326-5986-7 (paperback) | ISBN 978-1-5326-5987-4 (hardcover) | ISBN 978-1-5326-5988-1 (ebook)

Subjects: LCSH: Nudity. | Human body—Religious aspects—Christianity. | Christianity and culture.

Classification: BT741.3 T50 2019 (print) | BT741.3 (ebook)

Title page graphic by: www.Vecteezy.com

Manufactured in the U.S.A. 10/24/19

When I feel very near God I always
feel such a need to undress.

—Charles Kingsley

Contents

Acknowledgments

To Steve and Susanne Parker, for your endless patience and support. To David Hatton, Don Dorman, Orin Dablemont, Bill Hughes, Carrie Crumrin, and G. S. Muse, for your help reviewing and editing my manuscript. To John Armstrong, Andrew Meyer, Andrew Green, Nathan Poole, Ed and Mary Sue, Jarrah, Scott, Dylan, Kyle, Kevin, and Lenny; you are my best friends.

Acknowledgments

[illegible]

Chapter 1—**The Divine Disconnection**

A friend of mine recalled the discomfort he felt when, while attending a Christian conference, a man in the restroom tried to make conversation with him at the urinal. He said: "He wanted to discuss the talk that had just been given, but the fact that we were in the restroom made it difficult for me. It felt wrong discussing all we'd learned about the faith while holding what seems to be the least faithful part of my body in my hand."

In his book *Tortured Wonders*, Rodney Clapp describes the seeming paradox of talking about theology during a medical checkup:

> [The doctor] asked me to stand up and lower my shorts for a hernia exam. It was then, as I tried in futility not to be self-conscious, that he chose to ask about my occupation. I told him I was an editor and writer. "So what do you write about" he said. "Please turn your head and cough." "I write [cough] . . ." He moved his hand to the other side of my groin and interrupted—"Turn the other way and cough."
>
> "I write about [cough, cough] theology." "Oh," he said noncommittally, almost absentmindedly. "Now please bend over and put your elbows on the table, so I can check your prostate." Theology, or thinking about God, who by definition has no physical body, usually is a highly disembodied practice. It links to textual artifacts (especially in the scriptures) and occasionally to archaeological artifacts. But it is not hard, when one is doing theology, to forget about the body. Maybe thinking and writing about theology, and spirituality, should be

> done in the course of physical examinations (although it would be hard to concentrate). That would keep us down to earth and aware of the bodies that we possess . . . There are, I learned that day in the doctor's office, few pretensions to angelic, ethereal spirituality when your elbows are on the cold plastic of the examination table and you hear rubber gloves being snapped on behind you.[1]

While I couldn't help laughing at both of these anecdotes, they represent a very serious chasm in Christian thought; that is, the underlying belief that the concepts of "body" and "spirit" are somehow opposites. Christopher West, who is known for his work popularizing Pope John Paul II's Theology of the Body, wrote, "Tragically, many Christians grow up thinking of their bodies (especially their sexuality) as inherent obstacles to the spiritual life."[2]

In seeking to understand where such attitudes originated, it helps to have a grasp on how the body has been misunderstood within the framework of Christianity, both theologically and historically.

Biblical Ambivalence & Greek Influence

For Paul the human form is a "temple of the Holy Spirit"[3] in one context, yet in another it hinders a more complete union with Christ.[4] At one point Paul even refers to his physicality as a "body of death."[5] To the casual reader, it can be hard to distinguish between references to flesh as that which is sinful, and that which is physical. Multiple passages which posit the "flesh" against the purposes of God further contribute to a seeming duplicity in the way New Testament writers esteem the body.[6]

The ambivalence surrounding biblical references to the body has certainly contributed to its demoralization within traditional Christianity. Yet a far greater contribution has been made through the influence of early church fathers and Greek philosophers.

In her book *The Unauthorized Guide to Sex and the Church*, Carmen Renee Berry describes two interpretations of Christianity that competed with the apostles for control over the emerging church: the Judaizers and the Gnostics.

The Judaizers taught Christ as the only means of salvation; to them, Judaism was the only way to Christ. Gnosticism is a philosophy that creates a false division between the spiritual and physical dimensions of our existence. According to Berry:

> Scripture was applied and misapplied in ways that separated the world into the material world containing the body, sexuality, and eventually women in the "bad" category and the spiritual world containing the mind, celibacy, and eventually men in the "good" one.[7]

In his essay "The Body and Spiritual Practice," James Wiseman explains the influence Greek philosophy, and its trademark dualism, played in the development of religious Gnosticism:

> Although it would be grossly unfair to portray Plato as unambiguously anti-corporeal, and although the major Christian authors who respected his thought did not appropriate it in an uncritical way, certain passages from Plato's own works and from those of some of his disciples did influence the Christian understanding of the body.[8]

Wiseman cites a section from Plato's *Phaedo* as an illustration of this influence:

> So long as we keep to the body and our soul is contaminated with this imperfection, there is no chance of our ever attaining satisfactorily to our object, which we assert to be truth . . . It seems that so long as we are alive, we shall continue closest to knowledge if we avoid as much as we can all contact and association with the body, except when they are absolutely necessary, and instead of allowing ourselves to become infected with its nature, purify ourselves from it until God Himself gives us deliverance.[9]

According to Wiseman, this Platonic philosophy was embraced by Philo of Alexandria, the Jewish philosopher who lived during the time of Christ. Philo significantly influenced future

Christian writers like Origen and Clement of Alexandria. Origen, who believed both his body and sexuality to be his enemy, reputedly castrated himself "for the sake of the kingdom";[10] and Clement taught that Christ didn't even have a physical body.

One of the bestselling books in Christian history, *The Life of Anthony*, was written about Anthony of the Desert, who never bathed so as not to expose the surface of his body. In fact no one ever saw Anthony undressed until his clothes were removed to make for a proper burial after his death. Thirteenth-century friar St. Francis of Assisi neglected to properly care for his body in the most basic of ways to avoid "indulging the flesh."

Gnostic Influence Continues

Despite Jesus' frequent declarations that marriage is holy, Gnostic influence continued to infect culture with a negative view of sexuality long after his ascension. Gnostics regarded marriage as sinful, and singleness was equated with godliness.

Partly influenced by such attitudes, in the fourth century, Pope Siricius declared it a crime for priests to have sex with their own wives. Both Siricius and his contemporary St. Jerome believed Mary remained a virgin even after giving birth to Christ.

The Gnostics also devalued women, as it was their bodies that tempted men to sin. Ninth-century church father Theodore of Studius forbade monks from having even female animals, insisting that by becoming monks, they had "renounced the female sex altogether . . ."[11] In the eleventh century Pope Gregory VII wrote, "The church cannot escape from the clutches of laity unless priests first escape the clutches of their wives."[12]

Pope Urban II, a contemporary of Pope Gregory, ordered any priest who violated celibacy to be thrown into prison, and his wife and children sold into slavery.[13]

To Augustine, one of the most influential extra-biblical writers in Christian history, the body "presseth down the soul."[14] Augustine became the bishop of Hippo, and believed the penis was evil, semen was cursed, and intercourse was infected by sin even in the context of marriage.

To be fair, early Christians saw the body at its worst: the average life expectancy in the Roman world was less than thirty years, malnutrition was rampant, and crime rates exceeded those of modern-day cities like Detroit, Los Angeles, and Oakland. In Antioch so common were missing body parts that they wouldn't draw much more attention than an untied shoelace would in modern times, and corpses were routinely dumped into the street. This all adds perspective to the contempt with which premodern Christians held their bodies, but certainly doesn't justify it.

Third-century Platonic philosopher Plotinus was so dismissive of bodily existence that he wouldn't admit to having parents or a birthday. Similarly, and a little closer to home, my great-grandmother Hattie refused to go out in public for the entire duration of her pregnancy to avoid the shame of strangers knowing that she had had sex.

From Plotinus to Grandma Hattie, the belief that the body and its accompanying sexuality is "bad," has injected ambivalence into the way we esteem our bodies, our body parts, and our sexuality. Such ambivalence causes us to question the very nature of our embodiment. As Lauren Winner puts it:

> We Christians get embarrassed about our bodies. We are not always sure that God likes them very much. We are not sure whether bodies are good or bad . . .[15]

Carmen Renee Berry writes:

> A friend of mine, who is an excellent preacher, recently spoke on Christian sexuality. He said, "I was taught two contradictory things about sex. First, it's dirty. Second, I should save it for the one I love." No clearer statement could be made about the dichotomy presented to today's Christians . . . Where did we get the idea that our bodies—and more specifically our sexuality—are unclean, perhaps even evil? With little clarity, we are often taught a mishmash of dismal decrees on our physical selves: that our "flesh" leads us away from God, and yet Jesus

> became "flesh" and dwelt among us; that our bodies are separate from our spirits, and yet, as orthodox believers, we hold tenaciously to the bodily resurrection of Jesus; the less sexual we are, the more spiritual we are, and yet God created both male and female with the declaration that it wasn't good for us to be alone. Contradictions abound in Christian thinking. And we, as individuals trying to live our lives as God would desire, are flipped and flopped as these ideas collide.[16]

Does the body imprison the soul, or does it set it free? Is it holy, or is it "dirty"? Is it sacred, or is it shameful? Is the body an inherent obstacle to the spiritual life, or is it the very expression of it?

Spiritual "Stuff"

When I think of "spirits," I think of things that go bump in the night—ghosts and goblins, angels and demons—none of which have bodies. So it makes sense that the word *spiritual* would seem distant from the body. Clapp plays devil's advocate on this point: "Angels are bodiless, so we intuit that spirituality must not have anything to do with our physical bodies."[17]

To the contrary! Because most of the spiritual realm is unseen, we've gotten used to using symbolism to convey spiritual truths; yet the body is the one outstanding exception. The body gives actual physical mass to the spirit. Flesh is the "stuff" that renders spirit visible. Without a spirit we are corpses, yet without a body we are mere ghosts.

Just as a completed ceramic sculpture gives material substance to what was previously only an idea in the molder's mind, the human body gives substance to the character and creativity of God's mind. According to Christopher West:

> We aren't spirits "trapped" in our bodies. The [Catholic] Church has always maintained that we are embodied spirits, or spiritualized bodies. Through the profound union of body and soul in each of us, our bodies *reveal* or "make visible" the invisible reality of our spirits. But

> the body does even more. Because we're made in God's image, our bodies also make visible something of God's invisible mystery.[18]

Indeed God's invisible attributes have been "clearly seen, being understood by the things that are made . . ."[19] As Pope John Paul II stated, "The body, in fact, and it alone is capable of making visible what is invisible: the spiritual and the divine. It was created to transfer into the visible reality of the world, the mystery hidden since time immemorial in God."[20]

The body reveals these mysteries by demonstrating the attributes of God in both form and function, design and behavior. The body teaches us who God is.

The Unknown Masterpiece

In his book *The Cells Design: How Chemistry Reveals the Creators Artistry*, biochemist Fazale Rana probes the cells' biochemical systems looking for attributes of God. He compares this to the process by which the identity of painters is determined by the characteristics of their paintings:

> Sometime in the early 1970s, a junk dealer came across five ink drawings while clearing out a deceased woman's apartment in London. He hung onto them for several years, after which time one of them wound up in the hands of a Brighton art dealer. Eventually, that dealer showed the mysterious drawing to Mark Harris, an art aficionado, who concluded that the piece might well be an unknown work by Picasso.[21]

When Picasso's estate refused to confirm the authenticity of the drawing, which became known as "The Unknown Masterpiece," Mark Harris was charged with a difficult task: authenticating the artwork based solely on its attributes.

Harris began by pointing out hallmark features of Picasso's work, such as the fingerprint rolled into the wet ink at the bottom of the drawing, and by comparing the drawing to authenticated works by the artist. By identifying stylistic attributes that had been associated with Picasso, and discovering similarities between "The Unknown Masterpiece" and other paintings by Picasso (such as "The Three Dancers" and "Guernica"), Harris was able to amass a large body of evidence to support the claim that Picasso, indeed, painted the picture. In other words, Harris was able to identify the designer *by looking at the design*.

If it is true that God's divine nature is "understood by the things that are made," then examination of the body God created reveals not only the beauty and elegance of his design, but also unveils countless truths about his nature and his goodness.

The Body as a Teacher

The body is a miracle. The mere act of waking up in the morning involves more complexity than all the technologies NASA has ever designed. The outer ear captures fluctuations in air pressure that are created by the noise of an alarm clock, translating these fluctuations into an electrical signal that the brain can understand. The eyelids are extended upwards to reveal a fusion of light and color, which the brain weaves into visual information that can be recognized by the mind. Then thought activates the brain's cortex, creating an electromagnetic storm that sends a nerve impulse down through the spinal cord into the muscles, which animate the bones and joints of the body. All of this happens so that the arm can reach, and the finger can extend, to nudge the highly coveted snooze button.

For these three simple movements to occur, trillions of cells must fire over a quadrillion signals to each other simultaneously, and each cell must understand what the other is doing. Even when the body is in a state of rest, each cell is completing a few million processes per second just to keep us alive: creating proteins, absorbing nutrients, transporting oxygen, and fighting infections.

In his book *The Greatest Miracle in the World*, Og Mandino wrote a "memorandum from God," in which he unravels the marvel of our biology:

> Your brain is the most complex structure in the universe. I know. Within its three pounds are thirteen billion nerve cells, more than three times as many cells as there are people on your earth. To help you file away every perception, every sound, every taste, every smell, every action you have experienced since the day of your birth . . . And, to assist your brain in the control of your body I have dispersed, throughout your form, four million pain-sensitive structures, five hundred thousand touch detectors, and more than two hundred thousand temperature detectors. No nation's gold is better protected than you. None of your ancient wonders are greater than you . . . Within you is enough atomic energy to destroy any of the world's great cities . . . and rebuild it.[22]

Zoom in on any one system in the body and you'll be fascinated at all that has to take place to make the plan work. Geoffrey Simmons, in his book *What Darwin Didn't Know*, describes the inner workings of the digestive system:

> Look at how we transfer sugar, minerals, proteins, fats, carbohydrates, and vitamins from our dinner plates to our mouths, down to the gastrointestinal tract, through the walls of the small bowel, into the bloodstream, through the liver, and ultimately to every cell in the body. Millions of macroscopic and microscopic processes are utilized. How does the body even know which sugar (and there are many types) to absorb, or which protein (and there are hundreds) goes where, when, and in what quantity? How does it know which substances are safe to absorb, and which should be ignored, quickly eliminated, or destroyed? How does the small bowel know how to cooperate with the 500 different kinds of bacteria that live in it? These are incredibly complex functions that work together—and only together—to maintain the health of an individual.[23]

Words that could be used to describe the inventor of this process might include artistic, imaginative, original, inventive, beautiful, clever, magnificent—even stunning. C. S. Lewis wrote "We are, not metaphorically but in very truth, a Divine work of art . . ."[24]

If such a cursory look at the body's design warrants such adjectives, what might an even closer look reveal?

Cell Theology

Advances in biochemical technique have made it possible for researchers to get a closer look at the cell than ever before, revealing biochemical processes that mirror God's character attributes at the molecular level.

The bacterial flagellum, for example, is a biomolecular machine that reveals his intelligence. It reflects careful planning, purposeful design, and complex engineering. This mechanism is made up of over forty different kinds of proteins that function in concert exactly like a rotary motor would. According to Rana, its "components stand as direct analogs to the parts of a man-made motor, including a rotor, stator, drive shaft, bushing, universal joint, and propeller."[25]

When harmful breaks occur on strands of DNA, they don't die; they are instead repaired and given new life. Damaged DNA is removed and then resynthesized. The technical name for this repair mechanism is Homologous recombination, but in spiritual terms *it's called grace.*

Homologous recombination is just one of many cellular mechanisms that demonstrate that forgiveness isn't just an ethereal concept that occurs in our spiritual "hearts," forgiveness is hardwired into our cells. The process of death and resurrection plays itself out millions of times each hour within the biomolecular systems of the body.

The resilience of the body demonstrates God's *grace*; the complexity of the body demonstrates his *creativity*; and the quality control systems that govern cell reproduction demonstrate his *reliability*.

Indeed, the designer can be known by the design.

The Body as a Symbol

Just as the physiological processes that govern bodily function have much to teach us about God, so also does the symbolic nature of the body. In his book *Reclaiming the Body in Christian Spirituality*, Father Thomas Ryan wrote about the spiritual significance of male circumcision:

> In Jewish mystical practice the covering of the phallus with foreskin symbolized humanity's tendency to cover over or to forget that our origins are in the loins of God. Thus the foreskin of the male child is cut away from the phallus, "and it shall be a sign of the covenant between me and you" (Gen 17:11).[26]

The penis as a symbol of being in covenant with the living God? What a far cry this is from the way most Christian men view their penises! Through circumcision, the penis actually becomes a prayer. J. Phillip Newell wrote:

> At different points in Christian history, if there had been a religious ritual in relation to the male genitals, it might well have taken the form not of circumcision, but of emasculation. Again and again the Christian tradition has failed to make a profound connection between our spirituality and our humanity, between the mystery of God on the one hand, and the mystery of the human body on the other.[27]

As a static participant in our sexual sin, the penis often makes us men feel "unholy." It is usually excluded from our spiritual life. Yet, realizing how often my penis is involved in sin reminds me that I need to pray over it at *least* as often as I pray over the other parts of my body. I also do this because I need to be reminded that my genitals, just like the rest of me, were crafted by God.

Christian blogger Ethan Renoe wrote:

> One of my theology professors would always say we postmodern people do theology like this: And then he would crouch and cover up his crotch, like an embarrassed child who had jumped out of the bath and been

> caught by the babysitter. We will talk about God in relation to anything but our genitals.[28]

Minister David Hatton points out the symbolism of the female body: "The woman's body has breasts for a *physical* reason: to feed babies; but also for a *spiritual* reason: to display our Maker's own nurturing nature (Isaiah 66:11,13)."[29]

In his book *The Names of God*, Nathan Stone makes a relevant observation about the Hebrew root of the name *El Shaddai*:

> It is quite likely that there is some connection between the name Shaddai and the root from which some modern scholars think it is derived, but in view of the circumstances under which it is often used and in view of the translation of another word almost exactly like it, we believe it has another derivation and a more significant meaning than that of special power. *Shaddai* itself occurs forty-eight times in the Old Testament and is translated "almighty." The other word so like it, and from which we believe it to be derived, occurs twenty-four times and is translated "breast." As connected with the word breast, the title Shaddai signifies one who nourishes, supplies, satisfies. Connected with the word for God, El, it then becomes the "One mighty to nourish, satisfy, supply." Naturally with God the idea would be intensified, and it comes to mean the One who "sheds forth" and "pours" out sustenance and blessing. In this sense, then, God is the all-sufficient, the all-bountiful.[30]

Stone goes on to provide an example:

> Jacob upon his deathbed, blessing his sons and forecasting their future, says in Genesis 49:24–25, concerning Joseph: "His strong arms stayed limber, because of the hand of the Mighty One of Jacob . . . because of your father's God [El], who helps you, because of the Almighty [Shaddai], who blesses you with blessings of the heavens above, blessings of the deep that lies below, blessings of the breast and womb." The distinction and significance of names here is quite striking and obvious. It is God as El who helps, but it is God as Shaddai who abundantly blesses with all

> manner of blessings, and blessings of the breast . . . The point is that the word translated "breast" in these passages is the Hebrew shad from which is derived Shaddai, the name of God translated "almighty" in our Bibles.[31]

Affirming the symbolic intention of the female breast, the prophet Isaiah had this to say about Israel's future restoration:

> Whereas you have been forsaken and hated, So that no one went through you, I will make you an eternal excellence, a joy of many generations. You shall drink the milk of the Gentiles, and milk the breast of kings; you shall know that I, the Lord, am your Savior and your Redeemer, the Mighty One of Jacob.[32]

Isaiah goes on to call upon the people to stop mourning Jerusalem, but instead rejoice in its' redemption:

> That you may feed and be satisfied with the consolation of her bosom,
>
> That you may drink deeply and be delighted with the abundance of her glory.
>
> For thus says the Lord: "Behold, I will extend peace to her like a river,
>
> And the glory of the Gentiles like a flowing stream. Then you shall feed;
>
> On her sides shall you be carried, and be dandled on her knees. As one whom his mother comforts, So I will comfort you; and you shall be comforted in Jerusalem.[33]

Even the Apostle Peter instructs, "as newborn babes, desire the pure milk of the word, that you may grow thereby, if indeed you have tasted that the Lord is gracious."[34]

All this spiritual inference about the body, and I haven't even started talking about sex yet.

Chapter 2—**A Red Light in the Bedroom**

Perhaps it is because the body, and not just our own, has gotten us into so much trouble that we have unconsciously come to associate it with carnality. Consider the battle we fight to stay pure each time we pass a sexually explicit billboard while driving, visit a website we know we shouldn't, or allow impropriety into our fantasy life. The guilt of our sexual misgivings has forged into our Christian ethic the belief that the body is at war with the spirit.

Even using the word *purity* to describe victory in this context, connotes that if we lose our battle against the body, we'll be contaminated by it. Carmen Renee Berry wrote:

> When it comes to our actual bodies, Christian discourse takes a dramatic turn toward blame. We have pointed to our bodies, sometimes referred to as "flesh," as the source of sin. Due, in part, to translation problems, our physical bodies and our sinful natures have been seen as synonymous.[35]

But it is not the body that contaminates us, nor is the body our enemy in battle. According to the Apostle Paul:

> For we do not wrestle against *flesh and blood*, but against principalities, against powers, against the rulers of the darkness of this age, against spiritual hosts of wickedness in the heavenly places.[36]

The addition of "and blood" to this passage indicates that Paul was using "flesh" to describe literal bodies, rather than man's sinful nature. Similar comparisons are made in at least fifteen other New Testament passages. As it turns out, the word translated "flesh" in these passages is actually represented by one of four Greek words which are used interchangeably, sometimes referring to the literal body in a morally neutral context, and other times referring to the carnal nature in a more figurative sense. Clapp wrote:

> Casual readers of the New Testament are sometimes confused by references to sinful flesh, especially in the writings of Paul. But an only slightly closer reading reveals that *flesh* is a technical term for Paul . . . The "works of the flesh" include such attitudes and behaviors as quarreling and envy, matters more of spirit than of the physical body.[37]

So it becomes clear that our battle is not against our body, or the bodies of others; it is the "darkness of this age" that seeks to contaminate. When Jesus presented adultery as a sin that can occur absent from the body, he implicated the *heart*, not the body, as the source of this transgression:

> You have heard that it was said to those of old, 'You shall not commit adultery.' But I say to you that whoever looks at a woman to lust for her has already committed adultery with her in his heart.[38]

According to Christopher West:

> As a result of sin, our experience of sex has become terribly distorted. In the midst of these distortions, we can tend to think that there must be something wrong with sex itself (the "body-bad/sex-dirty" mentality stems from this). But the distortions we know so well are not at the core of sex. At the core of sex we discover a sign of God's own goodness.[39]

Perhaps it is this distortion that has influenced some theologians to interpret the sexual references in Song of Solomon as mere allegories. Carmen Renee Berry wrote, "Whenever I've heard a sermon citing the Song of Songs, the preacher has always said that the book described the relationship between Christ and the church. I guess that's one way to avoid the sexual intimacy about which Solomon wrote."[40]

She goes on to say, "We Christians seem to be comfortable with body-related and even sexually related metaphors . . . We're for body talk as long as it's symbolic."[41]

Father Ryan wrote:

> Many think that sexuality will go away or at least become quieter as we grow spiritually. But the contrary is true . . . The sexual dimension of our beings and relationships can lead us into a sense of the holy at levels deeper than conscious understanding. Oftentimes people seem to be praying to have their sexuality removed so they won't have to struggle with it anymore. That is a denial of a powerful, creative energy that connects us to one another. We *should* be struggling with it, like Jacob with the angel, for it is a messenger from God.[42]

The Body of Christ

It is certainly fascinating to discover how the intracellular process of Homologous recombination reveals God's mercy, or how the bacterial flagellum reveals His ingenuity; but the biological function of sexual intercourse reveals the Creator's great *love* for us.

Christopher West explains that God created sexual desire to give his creation the power to love each other, as he has loved us:[43]

> [Christ's commandment is that we] "Love one another as I have loved you" (Jn 15:12). How did Christ love us? Recall His words at the Last Supper: "*This is my body which is given for you*" (Lk 22:19). Love is supremely spiritual, but as Christ demonstrates, love is expressed and realized *in the body*.[44]

West illustrates this concept with a story:

> I never met my father-in-law; he died before my wife and I met. But I admire him tremendously because of the following story. At Mass the day after his wedding, having just consummated his marriage the night before, he was in tears after receiving the Eucharist. When his new bride inquired he said, "For the first time in my life

> I understood the meaning of Christ's words, 'This is my body given for you.'"[45]

Consider the words of the Apostle Paul:

> So husbands ought to love their own wives as their own bodies; he who loves his wife loves himself. For no one ever hated his own flesh, but nourishes and cherishes it, just as the Lord does the church. For we are members of His body, of His flesh and of His bones. "For this reason a man shall leave his father and mother and be joined to his wife, and the two shall become one flesh." This is a great mystery, but I speak concerning Christ and the church.[46]

Our Creator gave us intercourse so that we could more fully understand what it meant when the body of God saved the soul of man. Christ sacrificially gave up his body, even to the point of crucifixion, for his church. A man and woman who sacrificially give up their bodies for one another actually re-create, somehow, Christ's death on the cross. If the word *somehow* seems too vague, consider that even to the Apostle Paul this phenomenon was a "great mystery."

In this respect theology is actually inscribed on our bodies.[47] Sex, therefore, not only teaches us how to love, but shows us even more about Christ and the Scriptures that point to him. *Sex is exegesis.*

But not all sex is like this.

A Red Light in the Bedroom

The Red Light District is an urban area in Amsterdam with a high concentration of legalized prostitution, sex shops, strip clubs, and adult theaters. The term originates from the red lights that were historically used to signify brothels. Many would consider it one of the most sexually "liberated" places in the entire world. But Rob Bell, in his book *Sex God*, takes a different position on the district:

> The Red Light District in Amsterdam is so sexually repressed . . . What is so striking is how unsexual that

> whole section of the city is. There are lots of people "having sex" night and day, but that's all it is. There's no connection. That's, actually, the only way it works. They agree to a certain fee for certain acts performed, she performs them, he pays her, and then they part ways. The only way they would ever see each other again is on the slim probability that he would return and they would repeat this transaction. There's no connection whatsoever.[48]

Rob is making the point that a spiritual connection is required for intercourse to be "sexual." When the people involved do not love each other, they are not "making love," *they are making lust*; and lust does not teach us anything about God.

Prostitution is an extreme example of sex that takes place outside of God's design, but sometimes the only thing that distinguishes the kind of sex they have in Amsterdam from that which takes place in a marriage, is the glowing red sign outside the door.

According to Christopher West:

> . . . it's significant that Christ refers to looking lustfully at "a woman" in the generic sense. He doesn't stress that it's someone other than a spouse. As John Paul observes, a man commits "adultery in the heart" not by looking lustfully at a woman he isn't married to, "but *precisely* because he looks at a woman in this way. Even if he looked in this way at his wife, he could likewise commit adultery 'in his heart'" (Oct. 8, 1980). In other words, marriage does *not* justify lust . . . The sexual embrace is meant to image and express divine love. Anything less is a counterfeit that not only fails to satisfy, but wounds us terribly.[49]

A friend of mine recently studied *Paradise Lost* in his college literature class. In this seventeenth-century poem, John Milton portrays sex as wholesome before the fall, and scandalous after. One of my friend's classmates, who also happens to be an evangelical Christian, raised his hand and asserted, "I don't get it, they were married before the fall and after the fall; why was their sex wrong after the fall? They were married so they're good, right?"

Wrong.

I believe Milton's fictional poem accurately conveys the shift that must have occurred in the way Adam and Eve esteemed their bodies. Before the fall they didn't have the capacity to objectify one another; afterwards they did. It was in this manner that their "eyes were opened."

I don't really believe that a husband who lusts after his wife is in the same moral position as one who patronizes a brothel. I am just trying to illustrate that regardless of the context, love that is not sacrificial, that does not put the needs of the other person first, but instead seeks to use the other's body for its own pleasure, is not love.

This kind of sex fails to recognize the profound spirituality of the sexual bond between humans, the unique phenomenon that even the Apostle Paul called a "great mystery." This kind of sex fails to create any kind of distinction between humans and animals, for whom sex is merely a biological process.

Born This Way

"Food for the stomach and the stomach for food" is a little proverb the ancient Greeks used to rationalize their lack of sensual control. The phrase reduced the body to the sum of its physical cravings. When you're hungry, "Food [is] for the stomach," just like rest is for when you're tired, and sex is for when you're lonely.

The phrase could be compared to more recent proverbs used to justify sexual immorality such as "if it feels good do it," or the title of Lady Gaga's 2011 album *Born This Way*. The problem with all these proverbs is that they reduce the human body to nothing more than a biological machine, void of any moral connotations. Rob Bell wrote:

> This past year my family and I stayed at a wildlife lodge in Africa. We would wake up early each morning and climb into a Land Rover with our guide, who drove us all over the "bushveldt" as the Africans call it, looking at animals in their native habitats . . . When you see biological need up close, so raw and so primal, you can't help but notice

> how strong it is. These animals are going to mate because it's in their DNA, their blood, and their environment. They aren't lying out there in that field thinking, *I just really want to know that you love me for more than my body*. They aren't discussing how to make a difference in the world. One isn't saying to the other, "I just don't feel you're as committed to this relationship as I am." Other than basic biological functions, there's nothing else going on.[50]

Animals *are* born that way, humans are not. Yet Gaga's album contains lyrics like, "It doesn't matter if you love him . . . Just put your paws up 'cause you were born this way, baby."[51]

Lady Gaga is a gifted artist, and has since converted to Roman Catholicism. Nonetheless, these lyrics seem to deny that we have a spiritual dimension to us that the animals don't have. She seems to be suggesting that for humans, like animals, sex has no higher plane, no greater cause, no transcendent purpose.

The Apostle Paul, almost as though he saw Gaga coming, addresses this worldview:

> Foods for the stomach and the stomach for foods, but God will destroy both it and them. Now the body is not for sexual immorality but for the Lord, and the Lord for the body. And God both raised up the Lord and will also raise us up by His power. Do you not know that your bodies are members of Christ?[52]

I used to think Paul called our bodies' members of Christ's only to demonstrate how significant they are, or to make us feel guiltier when we use them to sin. Yet the more I learn about the connection between physiology and spirituality, the more convinced I am that Paul's admonition is to be taken literally.

The Substance of the Gospel

Traditional Christianity tends to view the body of Christ as a merely social body, and biblical references to Christians as Christ's body are considered metaphoric. Yet Paul was much more precise in his explanation of this concept, referring explicitly to the physicality of our representation of Christ: "For we are members of His body, *of His flesh and of His bones*."[53]

When Christ ascended into the heavenly realm,[54] the same Spirit that had been governing his actions on the earth entered all believers.[55] This happened so that our bodies could replace his.

Father Ron Rolheiser wrote:

> The incarnation began with Jesus and it has never stopped . . . God still has skin, human skin, and physically walks on this earth just as Jesus did. In a certain manner of speaking, it is true to say that, at the ascension, the physical body of Jesus left this earth, but the body of Christ did not. God's incarnational presence among us continues as before.[56]

St. Teresa of Ávila, who championed a contemplative life through mental prayer, so aptly wrote, "Christ has no body now but yours."[57] Perhaps this is why Paul likened physical bodies to "tablets of flesh"[58] on which the gospel is written, or "earthen vessels"[59] by which God's power is made manifest. Our bodies are the *substance* of the gospel.

Quantum Intercourse

Studies indicate that men's sex drives not only tend to be stronger than women's, but also that male and female sex drives tend to be motivated by vastly different factors, many of which cannot even be pinned down. I believe God intentionally designed these differences in brain chemistry so that marriage could mirror his relationship with us. The imbalance of sexual desire between the sexes forces *him* to pursue *her*, just as Christ pursues his bride: the church.

The quantum principle of entanglement asserts that when you split a single entity into two pieces, no matter how far you separate them, each piece still mirrors the physical properties of the other. In the quantum world, the notion of making "two" out of that which was once "one" is physically impossible. Such is the case with the sexual union between a man and a woman.

Several neurochemical processes occur during sex that bond lovers to one another. Men produce a bonding agent called vasopressin, and women produce oxytocin. These chemicals give physical substance to Christ's assertion that in sex, the two are made one. This explains why sex that takes place outside of a lifelong commitment is so emotionally destructive. Attempts to make "two" out of what was once "one" are, both scientifically and spiritually, impossible.

The problem with pornography is that the same chemicals that bind us to a spouse in lovemaking, will also bind us to images on a screen. Brain scans confirm that the thalamus, which plays a crucial role in distinguishing real from pretend, responds to inner and outer realities identically.

Mirror neurons fire in the brain when the body is engaged in action, but they also fire when we merely observe the same action being performed by another. The neuron "mirrors" the behavior of the other, as though the observer were performing the action themselves.[60] Perhaps this is why Jesus said one only needs to *look* at a woman lustfully, and he's already committed adultery.

Sexual activity also stimulates production of the same chemicals that drug use does, which explains the addictive nature of our relationships. We have a *chemical* need for relationship, though sexual activity isn't required to meet this need. A sincere conversation or close hug from a trusted friend will trigger the release of dopamine in my brain. Although in seasons of isolation, when there was no embrace to be had, I have turned to Internet pornography, which mimics intimacy by releasing the same chemicals that are released through real world relationship.[61]

It is in moments like these that God needs a body, because I need a hug. Loving our God and loving each other are so closely related that the New Testament uses the same Greek word to describe them both.[62] If you want a deeper relationship with God, start by loving those around you. By loving their body, you are loving God's.

When I'm transparent with someone about my need for affection and they ask "how is your relationship with God?," I know

I'm not getting a hug. It is the polite way of being told I should get my needs met directly through the Lord.

Such individuals have removed the body from the Christian life and, in so doing, confined the gospel to the invisible, ethereal realm where it exists only as an idea, and does no one any practical good here on earth.

The tendency to divorce spirit from matter, coupled with spiritual socialization that posits the body as "worldy," all serve as obstacles to integrating one's body into their relationship with God. Why are so many uncomfortable kneeling in church to pray, or lifting their hands in the air during a worship song? Father Ryan asks, "Is it because we have been conditioned to remove our bodies from the expression of our spiritual selves?"[63]

Indeed, this false division breeds a religious contempt for the body which tempts us not only to exclude it from religious life, but also to hide it from each other.

Chapter 3—**That Famous Fig Leaf**

Scripture tells us it was a cool day in the Garden when our forefathers tasted the forbidden fruit, and, in so doing, ushered in the fall of humankind. According to Genesis, "Then the eyes of both of them were opened, and they knew that they were naked . . ."[64]

Alan Wright, in his book *Shame Off You*, explains what the fall may have looked like in modern-day society:

> Imagine sitting in church and suddenly, during the sermon, a picture of you appears on the big projection screen and all of the thoughts you've had that week are exposed for the whole church to see. One embarrassing thought after another—moments of silent lust, jealous thoughts about other church members, critical thoughts toward the people on your pew. Now if you can imagine that horror, you're beginning to get the sense of sheer terror that Adam and Eve suddenly felt.[65]

Alan's words illustrate that nakedness, in this context, represented far more than just physical nudity; it symbolized many other dimensions of exposure as well. The word *nude* is typically used when referring to bodily exposure, while the term *naked* is much more universal; it suggests exposure not only of the surface of the body, but of the *essential self*, which includes the body as well as that which lies beneath it. In this respect a person can be nude without being naked, and vice versa.

Whereas nude only implies a lack of clothing, naked implies lack in a much broader context. Used conceptually, "the naked truth" is the truth minus the lies that previously covered it up; the "naked eye" is used to describe what the eyeball perceives when not covered by a microscope or other mechanical apparatus. *Naked* is a term used to describe anyone or anything that has been laid completely bare. It is in this context that Adam tells God he is naked even *after* he had covered himself up.[66]

Initially, the bodily aspect of his, and her, exposure was not merely symbolic: Adam and Eve were both nude *and* naked. So what were they going to do about it?

> . . . and they sewed fig leaves together and made themselves coverings. And they heard the sound of the Lord God walking in the garden in the cool of the day, and Adam and his wife hid themselves from the presence of the Lord God among the trees of the garden.[67]

And ever since this disobedient duo reached for that famous fig leaf we have all been hiding—hiding from each other and hiding from God. We don't want people to see our wounds, imperfections, or weaknesses (the parts of our *essential selves* we keep covered), and we certainly don't want them to see us without our clothes on. So in approximately 4000 BC Adam and Eve covered themselves with fig leaves, and in 1721 the "bathing machine" was introduced to the beaches of Great Britain.[68]

Swimmers would change clothes in the privacy of a fifty-square-foot box on wheels, which was then lowered into the water. The bather entered the surf through the front door, thereby preventing exposure before, during, and after completing their swim. While bathing machines were most popular in the British isles, by the late nineteenth century such devices could also be found in the United States, France, Germany, Mexico, Australia, and New Zealand.

In classical antiquity swimming and bathing were done naked. It wasn't until the late seventeenth century that females began to wear swimwear, but men continued to wade in the nude until beaches were desegregated and "swimming costumes" became compulsory. By 1860 these "costumes" had become mandatory in the UK, and soon thereafter in the US as well.

Male nudity in the United States and other Western countries was not a taboo prior the twentieth century, when swimming in the nude was the natural default for men in the United Kingdom, and in most of the rest of the world as well. Since this time, the association between shame and the exposed body has traveled far and wide; even permeating one of the highest political offices in the United States government.

Draping *the Spirit of Justice*

I was strolling about an outdoor mall in Peoria, Illinois with some friends, and I spotted a statue that almost made me choke on the pretzel twists in my mouth. It was a life-size rendition of a majestic lion, most likely made of bronze or clay, whose testicles were insufficient to say the least. Lions have sizable sex organs, yet this one had the genital architecture of a rat. A friend informed me that the mall had so many complaints about the original statue, whose anatomy was more realistic, that the artists who crafted it were called back to grind down the testicles.

Similarly, in 2002 Attorney General John Ashcroft (a self-identified Christian man) spent $8,000 of taxpayer money to hide a statue whose breasts were exposed. *The Spirit of Justice*, an eighteen-foot aluminum statute of a woman that stands in the US Department of Justice's Hall of Justice, was covered with drapes. The *Washington Post* humorously called this action the "most talked-about cover-up at the Justice Department" at the time![69]

Such efforts at bodily censorship may seem over the top, but are these examples any different from artistic depictions of Christ's crucifixion, which invariably depict a loin cloth that almost certainly wasn't there?[70] If breasts on an aluminum woman are too much to handle, how will Christianity reconcile with the idea of a very real Jesus who most assuredly had a penis?

Cleaning Up the Crucifixion

Bible teacher J. Vernon McGee wrote, "He was crucified naked. It is difficult for us, in this age of nudity and pornography, to comprehend the great humiliation He suffered by hanging nude on the cross. They had taken His garments and gambled for ownership. My friend, He went through it all, crucified naked, that you might be clothed with the righteousness of Christ and stand before God throughout the endless ages of eternity."[71]

According to Ethan Renoe, the covering of Christ's midsection is an attempt to "clean up" the crucifixion:

> In many ways, the fact that artists have typically covered Jesus up while hanging on the cross has done a disservice to our perception of His scope of atonement. We are used to seeing Him, battered and bloody, yes, but at least with a shred of decency left and a towel wrapped around his midsection . . . We try to "clean up" the crucifixion.[72]

A friend of mine has a daughter who was recently asked to draw a picture from the Bible to enter a drawing contest at school. He wrote:

> What did she draw? Jesus on the cross, naked, with a penis. We don't have any such pictures in our home, but somehow she got the idea that Jesus must have been naked on the cross. She was right, of course, but we're not sending that picture in to the art contest. She didn't get his nose quite right.[73]

Shower Head Trip

The origin of clothing is made clear in Scripture; the first "outfit" ever worn was made out of flimsy leaves by a bashful couple in a perfect garden. Because animal skins and vegetable materials decompose rapidly, there is very little archeological evidence for the origin of clothing.[74] The oldest known woven cloth was found in Turkey and dated to around 7000 BC.

Notwithstanding, the practice of habitually wearing clothes is a fairly recent innovation in human history. In primeval times our distant ancestors, evolving in Africa and migrating into a world of tropical and temperate climates, were certainly naked most or all of the time. As humans expanded into colder areas, they quickly had to adapt artificial covering. Not long after, they also started adopting customs to govern what clothing should be worn, and when it should be worn. (It was then that the purpose of clothing began to shift from merely keeping us warm, to being used to differentiate class, gender, and social status.)

Nonetheless, some cultures continued to appreciate the body in its most natural form.

The ancient societies of Greece and Rome both embraced the practice of public bathing in the nude. In Greece, nudity was commonplace during sporting events and festivals.[75] First-century historian Diodorus Siculus records that the Celts (who lived in modern-day continental Europe and the United Kingdom) commonly fought naked in battle.[76]

Even as recently as the 1960s nude swimming was commonplace at the YMCA in the United States (this was before females were admitted), and in many US high schools as well. In some locales swimming trunks were not even allowed in the pool. This was not a controversial practice during an era that was far less likely to view "skinny dipping" as an erotic phenomenon, especially among classmates of the same gender.

Yet today very little opportunity exists for people to see each other naked in a non-erotic context. Public schools haven't required showers for at least two decades, and some schools are even considering removing showers altogether, because they are so rarely used.

A 2009 article from *The Oregonian*, "Shower Together at School? No Way, Dude," observed:

> It's a rare student who showers after sports or gym classes these days. A quick dab of deodorant and a dousing of cologne or perfume, and it's on to the next class . . . Communal showers—the awkward rite of passage into puberty—are a thing of the past. In fact, Oregon schools haven't required showers for at least a decade. The same is true nationally.[77]

The *New York Times*, in a 1996 article "Students Still Sweat, They Just Don't Shower," wrote:

> Students across the United States have abandoned school showers, and their attitudes seem to be much the same whether they live in inner-city high-rises, on suburban cul-de-sacs or in far-flung little towns in cornfield country.[78]

The article goes on to quote student after student listing all the reasons they would never shower, or change clothes, in front of their same-gender classmates. "You don't want to get made fun of,"[79] stated one fifteen-year-old boy. ". . . you don't feel very good about yourself,"[80] said an overweight student who used to race to the locker rooms after class so that he'd be done showering before the other boys arrived. "You never know who's looking at you,"[81] said an eighteen-year-old female from Illinois.

Quotes from these students' teachers only further illustrate the fact that students are changing the way they change. "These guys don't want to undress in front of each other," said a high school teacher in suburban Chicago. "I just don't get it. When I started in '74, nobody even thought about things like this. The whole thing is just hard for me to accept."[82]

An Illinois football coach said "These guys would play a two-and-a-half-hour game, and then they'd just want to go home, all muddy, so they could have their privacy. Used to be, when you get sweaty and stinky, you wanted to take a shower."[83]

Also mentioned in the *Times* article is a boys' tennis team that practices mornings before school at the community racquet club, just a few blocks from the high school. "But rather than shower at the club, many of the boys get picked up by their parents and driven back home to shower, and then return to school."[84] The article goes on to say:

> A generation ago, when most schools mandated showers, a teacher would typically monitor students and hand out towels, making sure that proper hygiene was observed. In schools with pools, students were sometimes required to swim naked, and teachers would conduct inspections

> for cleanliness that schools today would not dare allow, whether because of greater respect for children or greater fear of lawsuits.[85]

Mass contempt for public showers seems, to many, to be something which emerged only in recent history. Yet when the American Civil Liberties Union threatened to file a lawsuit in federal court over a mandatory shower policy in Pennsylvania, the lawyer who worked the case was overwhelmed by correspondence from adults who supported him. "People remembered their own humiliation. I myself remember moving from my little country school to the city school, and being mortified about having to take showers. But in those days, you did what the schools said, you did what the teachers said."[86]

One author, critical of the normalization of nudity, wrote:

> One of my worst experiences was being forced to swim in the nude in high school. This was a common practice in Chicago and other large city schools until the 1970's. You had a choice: either swim in the nude for four years of high school or take ROTC to get a waiver. Envision 30 young boys at various stages of puberty, with a wide variety of body shapes, lining up so the coach, in his well-fitted swimsuit, could take attendance. There was my dramatically overweight friend with his eyes staring straight at the ground and my other friend, a "late bloomer," just waiting for the inevitable insults about his manhood. There was also the constant anxiety that a pubescent erection could appear at any time. You could only hope that you were already in the pool when it struck. The reasons for this barbaric and hurtful practice were ill-founded—the need for hygiene, the fear of bathing suit threads clogging the pool or the desire to "build cohesion" between young men. Talk to any man raised at that time and you will get similar stories of shame and embarrassment.[87]

If it's true that prior generations were on their own "shower head trip,"[88] then that of the current generation is far more severe. I grew up in the era of Diet Coke and Jane Fonda. It was a time when "normal" did not mean you had to be stick-thin and there wasn't the airbrushing of magazine covers you see today.

Yet if, even in this more "innocent" era, people struggled with body image issues, one can hardly imagine what the pressure is like for teens today. Popular culture has created an archetype of physique that only a small percentage of the population can possibly live up to. The anxiety created by this phenomenon creates a social climate in which many youth view group showers as a form of water torture. The scrutiny is just too intense.

According to the *New York Times*:

> Modesty among young people today seems, in some ways, out of step in a culture that sells and celebrates the uncovered body in advertisements, on television and in movies. But some health and physical education experts contend that many students withdraw precisely because of the overload of erotic images—so many perfectly toned bodies cannot help but leave ordinary mortals feeling a bit inadequate.[89]

In a more recent *Times* article, "Men's Locker Room Designers Take Pity on Naked Millennials," Choire Sicha reports on the emerging demand for nudity-free locker rooms. Sicha describes the fear which drives men to slide their underwear on under their towels: "Each day, thousands upon thousands of men in locker rooms nationwide struggle to put on their underwear while still covered chastely in shower towels, like horrible breathless arthropods molting into something tender-skinned. They writhe, still moist, into fresh clothes."[90]

Bryan Dunkelberger of S3 Design, an architecture firm that designs locker rooms, told Sicha:

> In the last 20 years, maybe 25 years, there's a huge cultural shift in people that ultimately affects gyms . . . Old-timers, guys that are 60-plus, have no problem with a gang shower and whatever. The Gen X-ers are a little bit more sensitive to what they're spending and what they're expecting. And the millennials, these are the special children. They expect all the amenities. They grew up

> in families that had Y.M.C.A. or country club memberships. They expect certain things. Privacy, they expect.[91]

Mark Joseph Stern, writing for Slate.com, commented on Sicha's article, "While older men generally remain comfortable being undressed among others, younger ones insist on maximum privacy, pining for a way to strip, shower, and change clothes without even a flash of nudity."[92]

Why is there such aversion to nudity among millennials? In the article "Nothing to See Here: A History of Showers in Sports," ESPN sports writer David Fleming describes the sociological constructs that converge when clothes come off, most of which are far more pronounced today than in the age of the boomers:

> When stinky teammates strip down to their most vulnerable state, it conjures, for some, a range of emotions: their most awkward memories (middle school gym class), deepest insecurities (size), purest symbolism (baptism) and most ignorant defense mechanisms (homophobia).[93]

Kyle Scott, on his blog CrossingBroad.com, further illustrates how prior generations have less aversion to nudity than current ones:

> No one likes the naked old man at the gym, but we've come to accept him, almost celebrate him, as an artifact from yesteryear. Back in the day, dudes were cool with being naked around each other. When I imagine old-timey conversations, I picture two guys sippin' beers and sittin' with their balls flopped over a stoop, talkin' 'bout "the block." This probably isn't an accurate view of life in simpler times, but it works for me. The point is, being naked is a generational thing. I used to think it was an age thing, but I'm 30 now, almost 31—well into being an actual adult—and I still don't feel even a little bit comfortable having a conversation with a naked man.[94]

Nightmarish Spaces

In an article written for *The Atlantic*, "The Private Lives of Public Bathrooms," Julie Beck asserts:

> The public collides uncomfortably with the private in the bathroom as it does nowhere else, and the unique behaviors we perform stem from a complex psychological stew of shame, self-awareness, design, and gender roles. If you boiled this stew down, though, it'd come down to boundaries—the stalls and dividers that physically separate us, and the social boundaries we create with our behavior when those don't feel like enough.[95]

Beck reports that a study published in the *British Journal of Criminology* in 2012 found that women tend to be more relaxed in public restrooms, but men are far more anxious.[96] According to Sarah Moore, a senior lecturer at the Royal Holloway University of London's Centre for Criminology and Sociology, public toilets are "nightmarish spaces" for men.[97] Beck wrote, "The anxiety they reported was centered around 'watching'—being watched by other men, or being perceived to be watching other men—and that this watching was linked to the possibility of sexual violence."[98]

In an article for Slate.com, J. Bryan Lowder describes one of the unspoken social rules that have been created to address this paranoia about seeing, and being seen:

> As anyone who has spent time in a men's room knows, one of the consequences of this wariness is the urinal spacing rule, in which, as you approach a bank of receptacles, you must choose the one farthest from the person already peeing. To do otherwise is to raise eyebrows in even the most progressive of lavatories; God help you if, say, the two ends are taken out of four, and you must select a gentleman to whom you will sidle up. It's surprising one doesn't hear of more nervous breakdowns during the mid-morning, post-coffee rush than one does.[99]

Research has found it takes a man almost twice as long to pee when there is a man at the urinal next to him.[100] So prevalent is the fear of being scrutinized, or assaulted, by others while using the restroom that it's actually been classified as a social anxiety disorder by the American Psychiatric Association. *Paruresis*, or "pee-shyness" affects about 20 million people in the United States according to Steve Soifer, who is CEO of the International Paruresis Association.

Beck interviewed one such sufferer, Alexis Sanchez, who scans underneath every stall to make sure the facility is empty before attempting to conduct any "business." If she's not alone, she will "either wait for the person to leave, or pretend that she's already finished, flush, wash her hands, and leave."[101]

Soifer told Beck, "There's all sorts of routines" that paruretics use to cope. "One of the classics is, if you walk in after someone, you wash your hands until they leave."[102]

Beck concludes,

> Even for the rest of us, who don't suffer a clinical level of anxiety, the public bathroom is a place that has ingrained behaviors and social rituals—leaving space at the urinals, avoiding conversation even with people you know—that we've all experienced, if not daily at an office, than [sic] out in the world, at restaurants and ball parks and airports.[103]

Too Close For Comfort

In his article "The 12 Worst Guys You Encounter In The Gym Locker Room," Kyle Scott addresses the unwritten social rules of shared changing spaces. He satirically (but still seriously) references the "Too Close for Comfort Guy" who doesn't take full advantage of the available space between himself and fellow gym-goers;[104] and the "Doing [Stuff] Naked Guy," who "flings his towel over his shoulder and then checks his phone, digs through his bag, brushes his teeth, looks in the mirror, picks a scab . . . all things that can be done with his cash and two prizes safely tucked away inside a towel or, preferably, pants."[105]

Scott goes on to call out the "Check Yo'self Guy" who shamelessly plants his foot on the vanity counter and "starts toasting his nuts dry" with a blow dryer.[106] Finally, there's the "Guy Who Towels Off for Too Long," about whom Scott wrote:

> It takes me approximately 12 seconds to adequately towel off when I'm at home. Maybe a few more if I really want to dry my hair. In a gym, however, on the rare occasion that I need to use the shower, that time is trimmed down to no more than four seconds. Face, armpits, grundel, legs. That's it. The rest is on its own. You want to get the boxers on as quickly as possible. But not this guy. Not the guy who towels off like he's performing a ritualistic dance in the woods. No, no. For this guy, drying off is a form of expression. There are interpretive dancers less animated than him. You're not sure if he's just trying to be thorough or make it rain, but all you know is that it's taking him *way too long* to dry his back.[107]

Reading so much about pee-shyness, body shame, and shower head trips reminds me that things aren't much different today than they were in the Garden: Adam and Eve hid their nakedness behind a tree, and teenagers go home to shower. It makes me wonder, had Adam and Eve resisted the fruit, would there still be stalls in the bathroom and curtains in the shower? Or would the hypersexualized body consciousness that pervades modern culture have been usurped by a more wholesome ethos?

Chapter 4—**Farquahr Finds His Penis**

> And He said, "Who told you that you were naked? Have you eaten from the tree of which I commanded you that you should not eat?"[108]

In this particular context, God was likely using the word *naked* to illustrate that Adam and Eve were "inadequate." Not only was the context of this passage different than Adam's initial revelation of nakedness, but even the original language is different. In Genesis 2:25 (prior to the fall), the Hebrew word translated "naked" is *'arowm*, which refers to literal nudity. Post-fig leaf, the word Adam uses to tell God he's naked is *`eyrom*, which refers to figurative nudity, connoting helplessness and lack.

When that famous first couple sunk their teeth into the fruity texture of rebellion, they were laid completely bare. This allowed them to see, for the first time, that they didn't measure up.

The biblical account of the exposure Adam and Eve endured is not merely a history lesson; rather, it is a phenomenon that repeats itself in each one of our lives. As Pope John Paul II once stated, an "echo" of the beginning exists in each one of us. The experiences of Adam and Eve are "always at the root of every human experience."[109] At some point in our lives, though more likely many points, we've all had to make the agonizing discovery that we are naked.

Toddler *Au Natural*

I was at my next-door neighbors house during a social gathering when I noticed the cheek muscles starting to stretch on this little

Chinese girl. She couldn't have been more than three or four years old. As the dimples grew larger, the metaphoric light bulb above her head was steadily brightening. The skin on either side of her cheeks continued to crease until her mouth had formed a grin so mischievous it would have put even the Grinch to shame. Then, right there in the middle of the room, she dropped her pants and underwear for God and everyone else to behold.

When her pants fell the room burst into uncomfortable laughter, at which point the toddlers' grin, somehow, grew even larger (I was afraid her cheeks were going to rip open). She was certainly a satisfied consumer of all the extra attention her nudist behavior had procured for her.

Then her mom scolded her, and followed it with a light swat on her wrist to let her know that dropping her drawers in a room full of people was not the thing to do. The scolding was certainly not inappropriate, considering the circumstances, but it got me thinking about how all toddlers are nudists. Anyone that has helped to raise a child in any capacity can probably recall, at least a handful of times, their youngster recreating the San Francisco Marathon in his or her birthday suit whilst sporting a grin as wide as the Golden Gate Bridge is long.

Toddlers know what it means to be, just like Adam and Eve before the fall, nude and unashamed. But at some point in their development all toddlers, like the Chinese girl at the party, begin to learn the lesson that nudity has a proper and improper context. Just as in the Garden, someone will tell them they are naked.

I wonder if, sometimes, the ways in which these lessons are taught can send the wrong message to developing minds. Is a three-year-old capable of understanding that dropping her pants has gotten her in trouble because it was out of a proper context; or could her immature mind perceive that she was scolded because the parts she exposed are "bad" and, therefore, *she* is bad?

In his book, *Healing the Shame that Binds You*, John Bradshaw tells a story similar to that of this three-year-old girl. A two-year-old boy named Farquahr, while exploring his body, points to his nose and calls it by name. His mother is exhilarated and calls in

Grandma to share Farquahr's brilliant achievement. Responding to this positive reinforcement, Farquahr begins proudly naming other parts of his body: ears, eyes, elbows, navel . . .

> and then one day, one Sunday with all the family in the living room (receiving the preacher), little Farquahr finds his penis! He's pretty excited. He thinks that if his nose impressed them, this will really impress them. So he wanders into the living room and proudly displays his penis! Never has little Farquahr seen such action! Mom has him by the ear, and he's moving faster than he's ever moved before. Her face is contorted. She is visibly shaken and tells him in no uncertain terms never to show himself off again. He's told that what he did was bad! . . . Variations of this scenario happen in the best of families. Parents who have had their own sexuality shamed cannot handle their children's sexuality. When their child explores his sexuality, parents react with disappointment or worse, disgust. Global comments such as "That's bad," "Don't ever touch yourself there," "Go get decent—put on your clothes," or "Cover your privates" link sexuality to something bad, dirty and disgusting. This part of us must be disowned.[110]

Sociologist Charles H. Cooley coined the term *looking-glass self* to describe how identity is created during the formative years of life. Children carefully observe how others react to their behaviors and then, based on how these reactions are perceived, the child shifts his or her identity to match. In other words, small children see themselves the way they believe others see them.

George Herbert Mead, a sociological contemporary of Cooley's, believed that a person's concept of mind and self are formed through early childhood social interactions, seeing ourselves as others do. He called it "taking the role of the other."[111]

The problem with this process is that it is hopelessly subjective. Children don't have the ability to accurately assess what others think of them, and their behavior. Many adults don't even have this ability. Bradshaw explains the egocentric (or "self-focused") nature of a child's reasoning:

> A very young child cannot understand that his dad is a sick alcoholic. Children are limited in logical ability. Their earliest way of thinking is through feelings. Children are also egocentric. This doesn't mean they are selfish in the usual meaning of the word. They are not morally selfish. Egocentric thinking means that a child will take everything personally. Even if a parent dies, a child can personalize it. A child might say something like, "If mommy had really loved me, she would not have gone to God's house; she would have stayed with me."[112]

This phenomenon makes it very easy for children to take words that were only meant to reject a behavior, as rejection of their essential selves. Negative feedback that is directed towards a child's gender or sexuality can be especially traumatizing; whether it is truly abuse or merely the child's egocentric misunderstanding doesn't matter. As Bradshaw states, shaming a child for something as instinctual as their sexuality is like "an acorn going through excruciating agony for becoming an oak, or a flower feeling ashamed for blooming."[113]

Generations of Betrayal

Learning to love our bodies starts young, when children can be taught to appreciate the stuff of which they're made. Yet no two words instill more fear and trembling in the mind of a parent than "The Talk." It is often a parent's discomfort with their own body that accounts for such anxiety when discussing the body of another. Children have a keen ability to sense this, and so the parent's body shame is passed onto the child, and it goes on through infinite generations. Bradshaw wrote: "Parents who have had their own sexuality shamed cannot handle their children's natural sexuality."[114]

For some parents the task of talking to their kids about the sexual purpose of their body is so terrifying that they opt out of it altogether. Relationship blogger Jayson Gaddis wrote, "To not teach children about the sacredness of their bodies and their sexuality is one of the CORE abandonments of our time."[115] Gaddis describes how parents' inability to talk to their kids about sex has left the task up to their peers, who are "equally as ashamed, misinformed, and confused." Gaddis wrote:

> I was completely and utterly abandoned, as was my father by his father and on and on. I get that it wasn't my Dad's fault. How could he teach me anything about sex given what was taught to him by a Dad who probably never even mentioned it? Generations of betrayal. Generations of neglect and looking the other way, hoping kids would "figure it out" or innocently thinking it would take care of itself.[116]

I was traumatized by the process of becoming an adolescent; by the fear of uncertainty and shame of secrecy, as to what changes were taking place in my body. Researching this book has surfaced many of my deep wounds in this regard. Many times I've had to step away from the keyboard to get on my knees and weep before the Lord. So many, like me, were never taught what our bodies are for, and promiscuity is our failed attempt to figure it out. Sexual indiscrimination is the fruit of our confusion.

According to Gaddis:

> Like it or not, the state of male sexuality in this culture (and probably the world) is that of a sick, neglected, and deeply abandoned child, and we can see the wake of it everywhere in our lives. The way boys treat girls, the way men treat women. The way boys treat boys. The bullying and shame, coercion, and intimidation to be a certain way sexually. The gay jokes, the "small penis" jokes, the "pussy" jokes, the rape, misogyny, misandry, the violence, Matthew Shepard, Penn State, Steubenville Rape, The Catholic Church, and the shame and self-hatred toward our own bodies.[117]

Snips and Snails

Hugo Schwyzer, a blogger for the Good Men Project, was sent the message at a very young age that "boys were dirty, girls were clean and pure."[118] He wrote, "I grew up hearing the nursery rhyme that claimed that little boys were made of 'snips and snails and puppy-dog tails' while girls were 'sugar and spice and everything nice.'"[119] Naturally, this paradigm extended to his body as well. He wrote:

> In sixth grade, the same year that puberty hit me with irrevocable force, I had an art teacher, Mr. Blake. (This dates me: few public middle schools have art teachers anymore.) I'll never forget his solemn declaration that great artists all acknowledged that the female form was more beautiful than the male. He made a passing crack that "no one wants to see naked men, anyway"—and the whole class laughed. "Ewwww," a girl sitting next to me said, evidently disgusted at the thought of a naked boy.[120]

Not long after that, Schwyzer had a few sexual encounters with men. He wasn't gay, yet found the admiration of gay men something to counter the perception that his body was "disgusting." Schwyzer asserts, "I was never as sexually attracted to my male partners as I was to women—but I was powerfully attracted to their attraction to me."[121]

Lack of information creates confusion about sex, and lack of affirmation creates shame about the body. This confusion, and conflation, informs our impropriety. But it doesn't have to be this way. Gaddis' example reminds me that there is hope for the current, and future, generations:

> I refuse to let other 4, 5, 6, 7-year-old boys teach my son about his sacred body. I refuse to let another kid shame him while he's naked or having hard core porn be his first sexual experience . . . I will show up for my son. I'm scared and excited to teach him everything about his beautiful body and its power. I feel inspired to train him to use his penis responsibly.[122]

Swords Between Their Legs

For victims of sexual abuse, even an orgasm may not feel "safe", especially if one occurred during their assault. The entire notion of sexuality gets inextricably fused with feelings of humiliation, shame, and sometimes even danger. Situations that involve undress may also be difficult for victims of sexual abuse, as nudity implies vulnerability, which in turn implies the potential for exploitation.

In the movie *Nell*, Jodie Foster plays a young woman who is raised in isolation from the outside world. When the town doctor finds her, she is hiding in the rafters of her forest cabin. She is scared to death, because the only other time males had entered her cabin, they raped her. Lacking a proper vocabulary, she knows only to describe the penises of her assailants as "swords between their legs."

Indeed, the bodies of those men *had* been used as weapons to assault her, and that is how she continued to view the male genitalia. After earning her trust, the doctor, played by Liam Neeson, convinces her to go skinny dipping with him in the river. He can think of no other way to show her that not every penis is a dagger apt to strike.

The fear of exploitation, while not unwarranted, may cause a parent to unintentionally impart body shame to their child. Correcting a child who displays their genitalia in public, or instructing them to "never show" their private parts to a stranger who asks, is good protocol towards the prevention of abuse. Yet this should be a *gentle* instruction, not an angry dictate. Adam and Eve responded to the revelation of their nakedness by hiding in shame, but this doesn't have to be the case for those whose caregivers can graciously correct misuse of the body, while still affirming its goodness.

Crafting a Vernacular

In 2013 the anatomically correct "You & Me Mommy Change My Diaper" doll hit store shelves, and simultaneously sparked a national conversation on how kids should be introduced to body parts. One outraged mother posted a pic of the doll's "goods" on Facebook, and received comments like "These (are) little girls that don't need to know the anatomy,"[123] and "Little girls should not be shown that on dolls. The company makes me sick."[124]

On her parenting blog SheKnows.com, Monica Beyer reacts to these comments:

> Really? It's a penis, it's a vulva—one on a baby is not going to kill you and it's definitely not going to turn your child into a pervert. Some people have them, others have something else. Hiding these body parts away is an element of a larger issue—that we are ashamed of our bodies, and that even babies are shameful. What happens when a child's mother gives birth to a baby boy? It's concerning that parents are so uncomfortable explaining a new or different body part that they'd rather keep babies blank or under wraps, and if an anatomically correct doll finds its way into a home, then it suddenly becomes a viral photo shared and re-shared on Facebook.[125]

Beyer would rather explain a doll's penis than give her daughter a false biology lesson: a baby that pees with no genitalia. She goes on to say, "How on earth is it inappropriate for a child to see a naked baby? What about a baby makes a penis or a vulva dirty or sexual? Because that's what it sounds like when people say that it's wrong for little girls to see it. The truth is, when a child points out the body part that she doesn't have, all a parent is required to do is call it by its name."[126]

Child expert Dr. Michele Borba told Today.com, "At ages 3, 4, 5, we should be talking to them with anatomically correct words: penis instead of pee-pee. You don't do that with other body parts. You don't call it your 'elbow-y' or your 'toe-toe' . . . We've learned that if parents are relaxed about this when kids are younger, then the child will feel comfortable coming to you with harder conversations later."[127]

According to Beyer:

> Some adults squirm at the mere thought of our children as sexual beings, which of course includes the future use of their genitals. However, our job as parents is to teach them that their parts, private or not, have a real name that they shouldn't be embarrassed to discuss. We don't make up silly names for ears or toes, so why should we for a penis or vulva—or give the underwear-area a broad term such as "down there"?[128]

Beyer interviewed moms on the topic and observed that many felt usage of the correct terms actually played a role in the child's safety. Vicki, a mother of two, said, "Proper names are *important* to teach your kids. Not only for educational purposes, but for safety. I need to know that my kids are able to articulate exactly which part is which in the case that someone might touch them inappropriately."[129]

Another parent wrote, "My wife is a DCFS [Department of Children and Family Services] worker and she's had to wade through too many interviews with children who can't say exactly where they were touched or with what because they lack the proper vocabulary. We want to be sure that our children know the proper names of all their parts, and aren't afraid to use them. Even if it does mean that some evenings out we have to deal with our 2-year-old asking everyone if they have two nipples, too."[130]

Usage of proper terminology prevents shame, increases safety, and curbs further confusion. Beyer concludes:

> Using proper names from the get-go can keep a lot of future confusion at bay. Take Shelly, mom of two, for instance. "When I was little, my parents referred to my vulva as a 'daisy' and a penis as a 'willy,'" she told us. "I distinctly remember being very confused the first time I was told that a pretty white flower growing in the field was also called a daisy. And I remember feeling awkward when I met a guy named Willy."[131]

"Just Me Vest and Trousers"

In their book *Sex Before the Sexual Revolution*, Simon Szreter and Kate Fisher provide an empirically based portrait of sexuality and intimacy within marriages in England during the mid-twentieth century. The book presents evidence from an oral history study which solicited firsthand accounts from eighty-nine men and women whose adolescence, marriage, and child-rearing occurred during the interwar and immediately post-war decades.

Among their observations is that children scorned for immodesty can carry the shame of exposure well into their adulthood. Horace, one of their survey respondents, said:

> I shall always remember . . . when I was 16 or 17 I came downstairs with me trousers [underwear] on. Just me vest and trousers. And he [father] gave me such a hell of a clout. He knocked me from one side of the room to the other: "You dare expose your body to your mother?"[132]

Horace recalled this event while explaining the embarrassment he felt when undressing on his wedding night in 1948. According to Szreter and Fisher:

> Many historians and contemporaries have tended to assume that social norms which encouraged the covering up of bodies inculcated a sexual shyness in young people which was productive of inhibitions, and difficult and unsatisfying sexual relationships.[133]

As a result of unhealthy body socialization, some of the wives would not even undress to have sex. Szreter and Fisher quote one husband who complained that, since his wife "insists on full clothing, [sex is] about as exciting as posting a letter."[134] Survey respondents Mark and Joanna, a couple who married in the late 1940s, had never seen each other nude even after forty-five years of marriage!

Adeline Masquelier, in her book *Dirt, Undress, and Difference*, points out that "in some European Catholic families, children until World War I wore gowns while bathing, lest they engage in the sinful contemplation of their nudity . . ."[135]

These stories further illustrate how profoundly children (and teens) internalize the reactions of others towards their own naked, or even partially naked, bodies. Allowing children to experience their own nakedness without shame is essential to helping them develop healthy attitudes about their bodies, and healthy sex lives later in life.

Allowing them to experience the nakedness of *others* without shame is just as important. If a child walks into the room when mommy or daddy has just gotten out of the shower, the reaction of the parent should be casual. A parent who gasps in horror, or scolds the child for making them feel uncomfortable, may unknowingly shame the child into thinking what they saw was "bad."

Familial Nudity

Parents sometimes avoid exposing their naked bodies to their young children, thinking they are somehow "protecting" them from the sight of a fully grown adult unclothed. But what are they protecting them *from*?

I believe the reticence of some parents to let their kids see them naked is the result of living in a culture that confuses casual nudity with eroticism. Parents who hesitate to disrobe in front of their children may do so because they don't want to wreck their child's "innocence" with imagery of a "sexual" nature. Yet by hiding their bodies, parents may be passing a tangled concept of modesty on to the next generation.

Children who are never exposed to nudity in the home, yet see it in movies and on television where almost every instance is sexually charged, become even more reinforced in the confusion that equates nudity exclusively with sexual arousal.

Socialization that teaches us, from a young age, that bodily exposure is inextricably linked with sex helps to create the stigma, and curiosity, that advertisers exploit while strategically framing their products beside immodest models. (Magazine and picture advertisements for liquor products in the Victorian era serve as an early example of this phenomenon. Women were shown with "a bit of leg" and holding a brandy bottle.)

Furthermore, a child who never experiences nudity outside the context of sex might be more likely to develop an unnatural curiosity towards the physique of his or her own gender; and that which becomes exotic in a child's mind has the potential to become erotic as they start growing into adulthood.

This was certainly the case in my own life; because I was almost always asked to leave the room when other males were getting undressed, I grew up thinking that the male body was something "secret" and shameful. This only added to my curiosity, thus forming the basis for my own struggle with same-gender attraction later in life.

Identifying with the Body

A child's ability to identify with his or her own gender is absolutely essential to healthy sexual development. A boy must see "pieces" of himself in other men, and a girl in other women. During normal development, this process happens unconsciously within the first few years of life. At birth, both boys and girls identify with their mother. They understand their existence primarily through hers. As they grow up, girls will continue to identify with their mother, and other women, into adulthood; but boys must detach from their mother and learn to identify instead with their father and other men.

This is accomplished as the boy is able to recognize similarities between himself and other males. A boy must discover that his male counterparts share in his interests, his insecurities, and even his physique. The following comment, posted on a fathering blog, describes how a boy can identify with his father's anatomy in a way that is free of bodily shame:

> When my son was little, we would shower together, so that I could make sure he was clean. He never wanted to wait outside of a bathroom for me, always wanting to

> come in, so he would always come in and we would use the bathroom together. Even as my son grew older, we continued this practice. In the fall of 2002 a change in my work schedule required me to get up at the same time my son awoke for school. It just didn't make sense for me to get up a half hour earlier every day to get ready before him, so I suggested to him that we share the facilities each morning. After all, I could use the extra half hour of sleep! I would wake him up each morning and then go into the shower. He would walk in a few minutes later, sit down on the toilet, and he and I would talk while I showered. When I got done in the shower we switched places. My son was 13 when this started and the "openness" of our morning ritual turned out to be a great help to him as he started puberty. We had many "birds and the bees" discussions in the bathroom. We talked about pubic hair, erections, masturbation, sex, and whatever else came to mind. My own father was never comfortable with this sort of stuff, so I had to learn it all on my own, which is why it felt so great to be able to be there for my son as his body changed. Even more recently (my son is now 21), we were in a Starbucks in Manhattan and the line was so huge that when my turn came, we just went in together, even though it was a single person restroom. It's really no big deal, we're both guys. My wife never had a problem with any of this, she always says "boys will be boys" and then laughs a little. A few years ago my wife and I had a daughter. I don't share the bathroom with her, in fact, it's the other way around; she shares the bathroom with my wife. I always wonder what they're talking about in there![136]

In his book *The Touch That Transforms*, Kyle Hamilton Barr retells a story that was shared with him by a friend who is raising young sons:

> When one of my sons was either two or three years old, he would say frequently "I'm a girl. I'm a princess!" At first, my wife and I weren't greatly concerned because we didn't really think he understood what he was saying. He was so innocent and it was always said in a joking manner rather than a serious one. Even though I would always

> correct him and say, "no you're a prince and a king," he would always revert back to his statement. When this continued to happen, I began to get more concerned. My wife and I then started praying and looking more into it. At that point, I remembered something that I had read from Tim Timmerman's book about a father and son going skinny dipping. So I thought that it might be good to do something vulnerable with both my boys like this. I wanted to show that he's part of us, the manhood, and what I have, he has; we're the same. So one night it was raining and the 3 of us jumped in our pool naked. We wrestled and I threw them around and enjoyed just being "dudes." Ever since that moment, my son became noticeably more confident in being a boy. He would say "I'm a boy!" all the time, reaffirming his identity. I think that day was pivotal because now if you try to tell him that he's a girl, he quickly matter-of-factly corrects you.[137]

I am not saying that sharing a bathroom or taking a skin dip with the same-gender parent will guarantee healthy sexuality. The dynamics of psycho-sexual development are far too complex for any single action to altogether prevent sexual ambiguity later on in life. I am merely presenting this as an important piece of a very complex puzzle.

As a child continues to grow and form his or her identity they will continue to identify with others of the same gender, although the context will change. Bodily identification will occur through culturally acceptable situations in which others of the same gender are not clothed, such as school locker rooms and public showers (what few are left).

Some adolescent boys may even "compare size" during the elementary and junior high school years. This is a very normal, and even healthy, process when it takes place among boys who are similar in age, and in a platonic context. Bradshaw wrote "Sexuality is somewhat awesome and confusing to a child. And children naturally explore their genitals . . ."[138]

A Pornified Culture

In his expose' on team behavior in NFL locker rooms, David Fleming wrote:

> Nether-region glancing in showers is so commonplace, according to scores of athletes interviewed for this story, there's even a crude term for when the eyes linger just a tad too long: meat peeping. Visit any locker room now or throughout history and administer sodium pentothal, and you would find that every player knows exactly which player has the largest, and smallest, penis on the team.

British sociologist Chris Morriss-Roberts conducted a study about locker room behavior. He wrote: "The research suggested that men look at each other's [penises], as a gauge to see how big or small they are, comparing themselves to the rest of the team or men in the locker room. The activity of checking out each other occurred irrelevant of sexuality and the type of sport; all participants noted that they looked at each other's [penises] in the locker room."[139]

Evolutionary Biologist Jared Diamond wrote that, for women, "the sight of a penis is, if anything, unattractive. The ones really fascinated by the penis and its dimensions are men. In the showers in men's locker rooms, men routinely size up each other's endowment."[140]

The "exploration" of which Bradshaw wrote, doesn't seem to cease when men grow up, but neither do media messages that suggest "real men" have the equivalent of a Mark 45 nuclear Navy torpedo in between their legs.

In his documentary *Unhung Hero*, Patrick Moote, who is admittedly insecure about his own size, traveled the world attempting to enlarge his penis using penis pumps, penis pills, and even penis calisthenics, to no avail. Moote asks internationally syndicated sex advice columnist Dan Savage why so many men are insecure about their penises. Dan replied: "We live in a pornified culture. Porn is a skewed sample. People aren't seeing a representative sample of penises anywhere, all they're seeing is porn penises."[141]

In her book *The Male Body*, Susan Bordo asks:

> Where do men get their ideas about how big their penises "ought" to be? Some . . . get them from a child's-eye view of their fathers' penises. Some get them from other guys in the locker room. Some become convinced they are too small because a partner has told them they don't measure up . . . But many men, like women, get their ideas about how big they should be from the bodies of cultural icons: the Dirk Digglers and Harry Reemses of video porn and sex magazines, hired specifically for their endowments . . . These guys are as off-the-charts vis-à-vis average penis size as the runway model is vis-à-vis the average female body.[142]

Bordo concludes, "If a Martian was planning a trip to earth and was given a *Vogue* and a *Playgirl* to enlighten him on what to expect from human women and men, he'd get a very misleading impression."[143]

All this hoopla about penis size ignores the medical literature that suggests a larger penis does not perform sexually superior to a smaller one. Towards the end of his documentary, Patrick Moote observed "The average depth of the female vagina is 3.2 inches. The average length of the male penis is 4.4 inches. So what's the problem?"[144]

Vanity, insecurity, gender ambiguity, performance anxiety; these are just a few, of many, legitimate answers to Patrick's rhetorical question.

A Creature of Imagination

Bordo takes a step beyond merely analyzing how culture connotes size, and posits the concept of *phallus* as the penile equivalent of the iconic (but non-biological) heart that appears on cards and candy boxes for Valentine's Day. The phallus is, according to Bordo "a creature of the cultural imagination, not biology."[145]

The phallus represents masculine ambition and attitude, a concept to which marketers appeal anytime they associate strength, power, or size with their product. Powerful engines, tall buildings, leather jackets; these are phallic symbols of masculinity.

Bordo wrote:

> The phallus is a cultural icon which men are taught to aspire to. They cannot succeed. Young men . . . have trouble seeing their penises realistically, and consistently judge them to be smaller than they actually are. In part, that's because it's not really flesh-and-blood penises that shape a young man's perception that his penis is less than it is or should be, but a majestic imaginary member, against which no man's penis can ever measure up. As psychologist Anthony Quaglieri insightfully notes, thinking that one's penis is smaller than it should be is not really about inches but "about how men are trained by the world to see ourselves as not enough."[146]

Small Arms and Artillery

Some men actually do have nuclear missiles in their pants (I've seen them in the gym locker room), but the rest of us need a little grounding. Both men, and boys, need a context in which we can see what real penises look like, lest those who just have "bullets" feel impoverished.

Having grown up outside of circumstances that would have allowed me to view the bodies of other men outside the context of sex, the Internet became the only place such identification could take place for me. I wasn't interested in watching sex acts, I just wanted to see what other males looked like naked, so I would know if I was normal.

I have actually counseled men who, while growing up, would look at themselves in the shower and think they must be deformed. Having never seen another male unclothed, they had no idea what they were supposed to look like. What an indictment this is on a culture that is removing showers from its school locker rooms!

Chapter 5—**The Pale Lover**

Those of us who live in civilized countries learn, at an early age, that there are sometimes consequences to exposing our body; whether it's a slap on the wrist (like the nudist toddler described in the previous chapter), or the ridicule of our peers in a group shower. Sometimes the reluctance to be seen in our birthday suits is the result of a purely personal preference, but very often it stems from assumptions about how others may receive the sight of our naked body.

According to Christopher West:

> A woman doesn't feel the need to cover her body when she's alone in the shower. But if a strange man burst into the bathroom she would. Why? The Pope [John Paul II] proposes that "shame" in this sense is a form of self-defense against being treated as an object for sexual use . . . Experience teaches her that men (because of the lust that resulted from original sin) tend to objectify women's bodies. Therefore, the woman covers her body not because it's "bad" or "shameful." She covers herself to protect her own dignity from the stranger's "lustful look"—a look that fails to respect her God-given dignity as a person.[147]

The woman in this illustration is suspicious of her body, or rather, suspicious of the effect it might have on someone of the opposite gender. However, a heightened awareness of homosexuality in our culture has removed any gender boundaries that once restricted this sort of suspicion. In the *New York Times* article I referenced earlier, concern about the presence of gay students was mentioned as one of the predominant reasons teens won't shower together.

Suspicious of the Body

My friend Tom recounted the almost traumatic embarrassment he experienced at a church retreat when he was in junior high. Tom had revealed his struggle with same-gender attraction to his youth pastor, who responded by making the entire group of junior high boys keep their shirts on in the hotel swimming pool. This was done to "protect" Tom from lusting after their exposed flesh. The pastor also made Tom share a room with one of the adult chaperones, instead of with other boys his own age, just in case he might have seen one of his peers changing their clothes.

A friend of mine, who made the decision to leave his gay partner and is now married to a beautiful woman, made a shocking discovery when he applied to volunteer in the children's ministry at his church. Even though it had been thirteen years since he'd been in a homosexual relationship (which had *never* included pedophilia), he was informed that the church had a blanket policy of not allowing those who had ever been in a gay relationship to work with children.

While I was visiting a good friend, Ned, for Christmas one year, he pulled me aside to say that he believed my relationship with his fourteen-year-old son was inappropriate. Shocked and confused, I asked what I could possibly have done to make him feel that way. He said that the horseplay between his son and I had become too excessive and intense. More specifically he was concerned that his teenage son, aware of my struggle with same-gender attraction, might misinterpret the intentions of my bodily contact.

How did my friend so quickly make the journey from horseplay to homosexuality? He, like so many in a culture dripping with sexual ambiguity, was suspicious of the body. But can I really blame him? The misuse of the body, in the context of broken or rebellious sexuality, has become so prevalent in our society that it's all we know to look for.

We are all suspicious of the body.

A Rite of Passage

The male locker room is a place that only men can go. For guys who struggle with same-gender attraction (and even for many who don't), the locker room shower symbolizes inclusion in, and acceptance by, ones gender. It is a rite of passage. (This is one reason the transgender community so covets the right to use the facilities that correspond to the gender they identify with.)

The transparency the shower facilitates, and vulnerability it requires, represents brotherhood, initiation, and a sense of masculine secrets shared. To be accepted among one's peers in the shower is to be told "you belong here, because you're one of us."

On his blog "The 4T's and the Church," Richard Padilla recounts a skinny dip he took with a group of male friends, one of whom knew that he was attracted to men, yet invited him to participate nonetheless. "I wanted to say, 'Dude, don't you remember what my struggle is?'" Yet his friend insisted on treating Richard exactly the same as all the other guys, despite his battle with same-gender attraction.[148]

Richard knew this was more than an invitation into a swimming pool. These men were accepting him as one of their own. They were inviting him into their world.

In a 2017 podcast episode titled "Physical Transparency," Padilla said:

> We all need to be seen naked. Its another aspect of being known. We know each other spiritually and emotionally, but I think that because of all the complexities of our sexualized culture we don't know how to embrace our bodies together.[149]

Three of Padilla's straight friends, Stephen Campos, Stephen Tanquary, and Matt Beckwith, joined the podcast and shared their thoughts on sharing locker rooms with same-gender attracted men. According to Campos, the first time he and Padilla showered together was awkward for both of them. "I thought we were gonna face each other and talk, but Richard was very quiet and just faced the wall the whole time."[150]

Padilla explains that, having never experienced nudity outside of an erotic context, he got nervous and simply froze. "When it comes to locker rooms people like me don't know the rules. We need straight guys to walk us into the locker room and say 'you belong here, and this is what we do.'"[151] Campos agreed: "There's a burden on the average straight guy to be open and inviting [to same-gender attracted guys in the locker room]."[152]

On his blog "The Silent Knight," A. J. Benjamin wrote of his experience moving into a dilapidated old mansion with a group of male friends during his college years. One of the guys in the house, Al, learned of his struggle with same-gender attraction shortly after moving in. A. J. describes being concerned that, following this discovery, Al might have reservations about using the shared bathroom in his presence. He wrote:

> . . . the next day we ended up in the bathroom at the same time. I had just gotten out of the shower and was about to dress when he came in. We exchanged morning greetings and he proceeded to undress as we chatted. Although the moment was only seconds, a healing occurred then. This man, this brother of mine, trusted me enough to be in the same room, in close corners with neither of us wearing a stitch, with him being fully aware of my struggles. This was one of the few times during the healing process that I actually felt something give inside me, almost like a snap. The joy that bubbled up almost made me laugh. He didn't seem aware of how deep this was for me at the time but his gift to me is one that I have never forgotten. Just having him accept me in both my literal and spiritual nakedness was incredible beyond words. Allowing me to do the same for him, was another brick in the divinely reconstructed edifice of my masculinity. It was the most profound of "locker room" experiences.[153]

In his book *A Bigger World Yet*, Tim Timmerman asked a group of men with unwanted same-gender attractions what has been most healing or helpful in regards to their sexual struggle:

> . . . They talk of being comfortable in their skin with other men, like when boys skinny dip or a group of guys hit the

> showers after a game. You may wonder, "How on earth can getting naked with another man be helpful? Wouldn't that just trigger the sexual desires all the more?" . . . Men who have difficulty seeing themselves as men need to learn to self identify as being part of the brotherhood in often the most basic of contexts: their bodies, that all men have the same equipment and they are an equal and the same as their gender mates. The nudity that has been healing to these men is far from erotic and is always in a brotherly context, free from sexual overtones. It is an inclusion of being "one of the guys" that this community of men has felt so estranged from.[154]

Tribalism and Community

Padilla's podcast addressed the role nudity plays in fostering community, even among men who don't experience same-gender attraction. Tanquary said, "I think guys being comfortable around each other naked is an important way for them to find community and acceptance."[155] Beckwith also spoke to the significance and symbolism of the shower: "There's a sort of tribalism and community that you have there that's really powerful."[156]

Campos, who played soccer with Tanquary at Biola University, said, "Being in the showers is probably one of my best memories of being on the team."[157] He goes on to recall one shower that was particularly meaningful:

> After the alumni game at Biola everyone hopped in the shower together and, I kid you not, it had to have been a 25 to 30 minute shower. We were singing, jumping, dancing, laughing, and joking. We burned each other with the shower heads.[158]

Tanquary, who was in the same shower, added, "When people tried to get out of the shower we would take soap and throw it at them, whip them with towels, etc."[159] Fleming, writing for ESPN, confirms that such tomfoolery has no respect to pay grades: "One of the most popular ways of hazing NFL rookies these days is by repeatedly splashing them with shampoo and liquid soap right as they step out of the shower, forcing them to go back inside to rinse off."[160]

A Modern-Day Milestone

The 2013 film *42* portrays the bigotry faced by Jackie Robinson, the first black man to play professional baseball, as he struggles to achieve inclusion and normalcy. There is a scene in which Jackie is shown waiting to take a shower when a fellow ball player asks, "Why do you wait for the rest of us to finish before you shower?"[161] When Robinson states that he doesn't want to make anyone uncomfortable, the teammate said:

> Take a shower with me . . . uh take a shower . . . I mean take a shower with us . . . ahem . . . you know . . . with the team.[162]

This invitation, and Jackie's acceptance of it, was a milestone of his integration into American baseball. ESPN reported, "The link between the regenerative properties of water and the masculine ritual of bathing together is so strong for teams that after integrating the major leagues, Jackie Robinson still felt like an outsider in his own clubhouse until a fellow Dodger coaxed him to start showering with the rest of his Brooklyn teammates."[163]

A modern-day milestone was reached when Michael Sam, the first publicly gay player to be drafted in the National Football League, stepped onto the moist, shimmering tile of the NFL's shower room, with the full blessing of his teammates. In so doing Sam was, according to ESPN, "breaking the ultimate taboo in men's team sports: an openly gay man showering with his NFL teammates."[164]

The Blue House

In 2004 I moved into a blue house with a group of my closest male friends. All straight guys that I had become inseparably close to in the years prior to moving into the house.

While living in the blue house, some of my male friends would not shower or change clothes in my presence, even while they had no problem doing these things with other guys. When I questioned my friends about this, some of them had assumed their modesty was "protecting" me. After all, they would struggle with lustful thoughts in the presence of a naked woman, so they naturally viewed my homosexual inclinations as being identical to their struggle, except directed towards men.

David Fleming asks the same question: ". . . isn't a gay player's showering with straight teammates the same as a straight man in a locker room full of attractive women?"[165]

For the answer, Fleming turns to former NFL cornerback Wade Davis, who says, "no, and when speaking to teams he asks straight players to imagine that the women in their locker room fantasy are, instead, their moms, sisters, aunts, and other family members. It's the same for gay players, he says: They view teammates as family. They're not going to be attracted to their brothers. And vice versa."[166]

Davis' response is spot on, yet many straight men still feel uncomfortable welcoming those with same-gender attractions into the shower. This is especially the case among evangelicals, many of whom have told me repeatedly that such a scenario is "inappropriate." (The stance of some Catholics has been that one is putting themself near the "occasion of sin.")

I can't fault my friends for doing what they thought was in my best interest. Yet the irony is that, having not completed the process of bodily identification that I described in the previous chapter, I actually needed to be included in these moments of undress *because* of my struggle with same-gender attraction, not in spite of it.

"It Moved"

While some of my friends excluded me from the shower with my best interest at heart, others excluded me for fear of being sexualized. Like so many in our hypersexualized culture, they were suspicious of the body. It is with this same suspicion that many men will accept sore muscles, rather than receive the healing that therapeutic massage offers. The hypersexualization of touch, coupled with fear of getting an erection, causes many to associate even clinical touch with feelings of guilt instead of relief.

A massage therapist who blogs anonymously wrote, "I get asked about erections regularly. By both men and women. Fear of getting an erection [during massage] is a powerful deterrent for men. Some aren't comfortable getting [a] massage from a man because they're afraid 'it will move' and some simply won't get massages at all for the same reason."[167]

The latter part of this quote is likely referring to an episode of the 1990s sitcom *Seinfeld*, in which George Costanza questions his sexuality because, during a massage he receives from a man, "It moved." What happened to George is a natural physiological response to being touched near the thigh. Nonetheless, this "movement" wounds the consciences of many men, some of whom will not return as a result.

The Cult of Hardness

In his book *A Mind of Its Own: A Cultural History of the Penis*, David Friedman explains that early Greek and Roman culture attached no shame or guilt to the natural phenomena of getting an erection. "For the Greeks and Romans, an erection was like a change in heartbeat; involuntary, and not susceptible to blame or praise."[168]

Somewhere around 500 BC, the Greeks celebrated their erections with statues called *hermae*. According to Friedman, *hermae* were "stone or wood columns topped by the head of the god Hermes and marked at the midpoint by an erection."[169] He goes on to say, "Like Athens, depictions of erections were everywhere in Rome—on paving stones, at the public baths, on the walls of private homes—promoting good luck or warding off bad."[170]

A look at the subtext that's attached to modern-day erections is enough to make one sentimental of the 500s BC. The mere notion of getting an erection in the locker room, and the weight of its implication, is more terrifying to men than everything but the notion of *not* getting one in the bedroom. A man's ability to "rise" to the occasion of lovemaking is a profound bastion of self-worth for both genders; affirming both his masculinity and her desirability.

Susan Bordo wrote, "The erect penis is often endowed with a tumescent *consciousness* that is bold, unafraid, at the ready."[171] Bordo refers to "the cult of hardness" to describe an ethos that associates hardness with masculinity: hard penises, hard bodies, hardness of resolve; as when Martin Luther said, "Here I stand, I can do no other." Kick-boxers, torpedoes, armored tanks; all are hard, and all are powerful. "To be exposed as 'soft' at the core," wrote Bordo "is one of the worst things a man can suffer in this culture."[172]

In a culture that esteems hardness over softness, strength above intimacy, armor rather than vulnerability, it's not surprising that Pfizer broke so many sales records by marketing its drug Viagra as though it were a sports car. Viagra was launched in the late nineties as an "impotency" drug. Bordo wrote, "Unlike other disorders, impotence implies the whole man, not merely the body part. *He is impotent.* Would we ever say about a person with a headache, '*He is a headache*'?"[173]

The Oxford Dictionary defines the word *impotent* first as "Unable to take effective action; helpless or powerless,"[174] and only secondarily relates the word to sexual performance. By positing "soft" men as powerless, and equating Viagra with "performance," the drug restored pride to damaged egos. (Though some still assert that "sex can never be deeply satisfying to men so long as it is viewed as a test of potency and performance."[175])

The term *impotence* has since been replaced with the more clinical term: *erectile dysfunction*. But the drug's purpose hasn't changed. For the majority of men, Viagra was never about reproduction, it was about vanity. Despite whatever psychological issues were plaguing a couple's sex life, Viagra promised to fix it with a simple tweak to the hydraulics.

As long as men conflate sexual performance with masculine identity, they will continue to be enchanted by Viagra; using sexual performance to compensate for more intrinsic issues. Even if a man can't have a hard body, nor hardness of will, at least Viagra can give him a hard penis.

Eroticizing Nudity

The circumstances in which nudity can occur outside of a sexual context are becoming more and more elusive, as is indicated by the disposition of many adolescents and millennials towards communal showers. Yet bodies that are, at least partially, exposed for the purpose of sensual gratification are everywhere. We live in a culture whose inhabitants spend billions of dollars a year to see each other naked on Internet sites and in pornographic films, yet are often uncomfortable changing in front of each other in locker rooms or even being seen in a swimsuit on the beach. This is due to either bodily insecurity, or fear of being sexually objectified.

Could it be that we have so profoundly fused the image of the exposed body with sexual gratification that there is no context left for it to be laid bare without evoking either shame or arousal?

According to Christopher West: "Since lust so often holds sway in our fallen world, nakedness is often intertwined with all that is not holy."[176]

The excessive number of Christians addicted to pornography (up to 50 percent by some estimates)[177] is often stated as though it's an oxymoron. Christians should be expected to struggle less since our faith prohibits such behavior, or so goes the logic. Yet I believe at least a portion of pornography's appeal is *because* of these prohibitions.

The sinful nature of lust contributes to its pleasure. The more forbidden the behavior, the more erotic it becomes. Why else would so many sexually themed web sites refer to their models as "naughty"?

American filmmaker John Waters was asked what inspired him to make a particular NC-17 film, to which he replied, "I think it was when I was eight years old [and] all the nuns told me I'd go to hell if I watched sexploitation movies. So naturally I became obsessed."[178]

In the same interview Waters almost seems to thank his uptight conservative parents for such strict Catholic upbringing, because it made sex more shameful and, therefore, more fun:

> When you're brought up to think that sex is dirty, it will always be better because dirty sex *is* better. Sex can't be that wholesome or it gets really boring. I liked doing it when it was illegal. Just think, every time you had sex, you broke the law! It's so much more fun that way.[179]

Consider a man being aroused by a bikini-clad female on the beach. How much more exciting would it be for him if he spotted this same woman in her underwear through the window of her home at night? The fact that the latter is forbidden would make the experience far more erotic for most men, even though the woman's undergarments cover precisely the same areas of her body that a swimsuit would.

Accordingly, the Christian ethos that views the naked body as something "not holy" creates feelings of shame that cause many to view even casual nudity as "naughty." This spiritual shame contributes significantly to the eroticization of the body.

A Pornographic View

In his book *Meeting at the River*, Hatton wrote: "Porn addiction in society, and in the church as well, is planted by a sexualized view of the body and nourished by a legalistic enforcement of that view."[180]

Hatton's book is written as a fictional story in which he encounters a group of Bible college students skinny dipping in the woods. When they emerge from the water, a lively dialogue ensues about the theological implications of nudity. For his part, Hatton asserts that the conflation of nudity with transgression has created a "pornographic view" of the body that only strengthens the chains of bondage to pornography. Enforcing the taboo of nudity only promotes the very problem it promised to solve. Hatton expounds:

> When people teach that the human body is dirty or obscene, it creates fertile ground for pornography. This is why porn addiction is so strong in our society, even among Christians. Our culture is inundated with a sexualized view of the body. I'm sorry to say that the church has been a key player in spreading that idea . . . But the church is trying to fight fire with gasoline . . . [because a] prudish view of the body is a pornographic one . . .[181]

Hatton continues:

> Those preaching this taboo often imagine the nude body to be a moral stumbling block, when, on the contrary, this concept itself is one of the biggest stumbling blocks over which our young people trip and fall into sexual impurity . . . because the perpetually covered body prevents a wholesome satisfaction of the curiosity it unnaturally creates.[182]

Hatton goes on to say that both pornographers and preachers speak the same sexual language about nakedness: the latter banning it as sexual sin, the former selling it for sexual lust.[183] "Prudery hides the body . . . pornography flaunts it."[184] According to Hatton, both approaches esteem nudity the same way: "*indecent, obscene, lustful.*"[185]

Most Christian books posit bodily exposure as an exploitation in any context but marriage. Their seams burst with techniques to prevent an unwholesome gaze at the body, yet no allowance is made for a *wholesome* view to take it's place.

Some would make exceptions for physicians, morticians, and sculptors, but, for the most part, the evangelical purity movement is wholly about closing one's eyes to that which is bad, not opening them up to that which is *good.* With only rare exceptions, the Christian purity movement conflates prudery with purity, and nudity with lust.

On the other hand, creating an atmosphere more accepting of non-sexual nudity will diminish the allure of pornography, and help both young and old esteem their body as a sanctuary for God's presence, rather than the object of carnality. One of the characters in Hattons' fictional dialogue summarizes the concept:

> . . . being accepted in your humble nakedness, by friends and family and others, is healing. It breaks the bondage to ungodly shame over the size or shape or blemishes of the body that God has given you.[186]

Hatton isn't a nudist (and neither am I). He's merely suggesting that culturally appropriate instances of undress should be embraced instead of scorned. This acceptance might look like two friends taking a skinny dip in a private pool, or simply changing into swimsuits openly and without shame (instead of facing the wall to avoid exposure).

I have also had healthy encounters with nudity in places where it occurs naturally, like gym showers, Korean spas, and nude beaches; all places where the body is exposed, but not sexualized. Just like Hatton, I have found that, rather than creating the problem of lust, such wholesome expression of bodily acceptance solves it.

A Glimpse of the Garden

I can remember playing with toys in my grandparent's basement as a small child when my grandfather walked out of the shower. I looked at his body because I wanted to see if it looked like mine but, instead of being affirmed, I was scolded. This experience etched itself into the wet concrete of my developing mind and, from that moment on, I viewed the masculine physique as something that was both shameful and profoundly mystical.

Just like the man watching the underwear-clad female through her bedroom window, the perception that my grandfather's body was "bad" only intensified my desire to see other men naked. When I hit puberty about a decade later, this shame became the driving force behind my struggle with homosexual lust.

This process not only explains how I was conditioned, as a small boy, to become aroused by the bodies of other men, but also illuminates the cause of a fetish I developed later on in life. When looking for pictures of naked men on the Internet, I was especially struck by those in which the models were smiling, because it meant they weren't mad at me for looking at their bodies. Their friendly disposition confirmed that I didn't have to fear getting in trouble for what I had seen. The men in the photos were naked, *and that was ok with them.* These smiling men represented the antithesis of the scolding I had received from my grandfather.

Not long after viewing these photos I went to visit my younger brother at Greenville College (now University) in Illinois. Using the communal showers in the freshmen dorms represented the first time I had seen a man naked without getting scolded. I was fascinated by how comfortable these men were being naked in front of each other: nudity without pretense. They were just guys being guys.

No, *we* were just guys being guys.

Male nudity in the context of shame had always incited me to lust; but nudity in the context of camaraderie had short-circuited the feelings of arousal and starved the fantasies that typically followed. On that day God began reconditioning my mind to associate the masculine physique with beauty and innocence, instead of secrecy and shame.

Timmerman wrote:

> Men who struggle with sexualizing their same gender have a false sense that men are "the other" rather than women, so when naked in a non-sexual context, they are confronted with the fact that they have the same equipment and they are part of a larger community of men. In the right context, that camaraderie dilutes and negates any sexualizing that could take place . . . Another aspect is many of these men who struggle with their sexuality have experienced painful and traumatic events in public or private settings when they were nude, like sexual

> abuse, shaming words about their body from adults or others, or agonizing events in the high school locker room. Many of the men I know have *never* been in a context where they could feel equal in body with other boys or men in a safe non-sexual or [non-]abusive setting. Being naked in a context with men who are safe or, even better yet, intimate friends can be an extraordinary redemptive event of equality and healing.[187]

The showers at Greenville College may not have given me the full revelation of what life was like before the fall, but on that day God had given me just a glimpse of what it meant to be naked and unashamed. God had given me just a glimpse of the Garden.

The Roots of Attraction

Understanding how the experience with my grandfather had informed my struggle with lust provided a framework for me to overcome it. If the Holy Spirit was able to surface the areas of woundedness and confusion that had broken my sexuality, he will certainly do it for others.

Whether a person is struggling with lust towards the same gender, the opposite gender, animals, inanimate objects, or anything else, there is value in exploring the unresolved emotional issues that inform unsanctified sexual desire. Doing so can lead to much greater freedom than the avoidance techniques prescribed by most Christian books on sexual addiction.

Superficial changes like installing a porn filter, or vowing to call a friend when desire strikes, succeed in preventing external manifestation of sexual sin, but they fail to address the internal reasons that one desires such things to begin with. One Christian website even suggests men overcome pornography addiction by vowing to pick up trash on the highway or send money to a rival political party each time they succumb.[188] Such techniques modify behavior, but our hearts remain evil.

Many evangelical leaders have encouraged gay-oriented individuals to seek the deep roots of their disparate attractions through intensive counseling and fervent prayer. Yet the heterosexual male whose orientation is towards objectification, voyeurism, or bondage is merely instructed to move his computer into a public space and read his Bible more. This advice is not only inadequate, but also doubles the standard for those who lust after their own gender, thus solidifying the notion that, among evangelicals, heterosexual lust doesn't hold the same gravity as homosexual lust.

Boobs are a Bonus

A 2009 Princeton University study questioned twenty-one heterosexual male undergraduates to discover how their brains perceived scantily clad women. The study found that, while viewing a woman in a bikini, the same region of the brain lit up that would become active when handling tools (such as a screwdriver or a wrench).[189]

Some of the men in the study showed no brain activity whatsoever in the medial prefrontal cortex, the part of the brain that activates when considering the thoughts and feelings of another. This research suggests that a man looking at a woman who is nude, or provocatively dressed, sees her as nothing more than an object to be used.

Sexuality that relies solely on the body for arousal is broken. The body was not designed to be enjoyed apart from the spirit that resides inside. This is why prostitution is not merely the exploitation of one's body; it is the exploitation of their soul.

I was recently explaining to a friend that it is not objectification to appreciate the body within the context of the soul. My comment to him was, "Its only objectification when you're aroused by the body in isolation." He humorously responded, "Boobs are a bonus in conjunction to the soul!"

An Ethos of Objectification

The sexual entertainment industry has so profoundly divorced physical intimacy from the spirit of the person being exploited, that their soul isn't even needed to complete the transaction, just the package it's wrapped in. In this context, pornography use and prostitution are not that distant from each other; the instigator of either is merely a *consumer* of the body.

Melinda Tankard Reist, cofounder of Collective Shout, wrote, "Growing up in a pornified landscape, girls learn that they are service stations for male gratification and pleasure."[190] Reist goes on to explain the impact male pornography use has on adolescent females:

> Girls describe being ranked at school on their bodies, and are sometimes compared to the bodies of porn stars. They know they can't compete, but that doesn't stop them thinking they have to. Requests for labia-plasty [cosmetic surgery that altars the appearance of the genital area] have tripled in a little over a decade among young women aged 15–24. Girls who don't undergo porn-inspired "Brazilian" waxing are often considered ugly or ungroomed (by boys as well as by other girls).[191]

Consistent with the ethos of objectification, young males commonly ask their sexual partners to send photos of their breasts and genitalia. Reist wrote that girls "are tired of being pressured for images they don't want to send, but they seem resigned to how normal the practice has become. Boys use the images as a form of currency, to swap and share and to use to humiliate girls publicly."[192]

Indeed young males, and some females, disseminate these pictures without consent to spite their enemies or humiliate former partners. The practice, appropriately labeled "revenge porn," has been linked to several suicides and has even been used to blackmail minors. Perpetrators obtain the images by posing as other youth on social media sites, then ask the victim to "trade pics."

The Pale Lover

In *Mere Christianity*, C. S. Lewis uses food as a metaphor to illustrate the sin of objectification:

> You can get a large audience together for a strip-tease act—that is, to watch a girl undress on the stage. Now suppose you came to a country where you could fill a theatre by simply bringing a covered plate on to the stage and then slowly lifting the cover so as to let every one see, just before the lights went out, that it contained a mutton chop or a bit of bacon, would you not think that in that country something had gone wrong with the appetite for food?[193]

Rodney Clapp provides a description of sexual arousal that transcends the appearance of the body:

> My lover lay in bed pale, weeping, maybe feverish, consumed by her flu or another malady. I lay down beside her and held her in my arms, really wanting the best for her: that she be well for her own sake. Her forehead on my shoulder, the smooth small of her back under my stroking fingers, her silken hair in my nose and eyes—these were all beautiful and good, as true as dawn after a desperate night. And holding and caressing her was an act of pure, grateful love, that her beauty is freely shared with and offered to me and that it, with her health, should be restored to its fullness. After a few minutes, I gradually realized I was aroused . . . Her beauty was beauty, true beauty. Rightly ordered desires are aroused by true beauty.[194]

Only a man who's learned to enjoy the body in relation to the soul could make a virus sufferer sound so elegant! Rodney's wife may have been throwing up profusely with terrible breath and bags under her eyes, but her beauty, to him wasn't so connected to the condition of her body that its temporary malformation reduced its appeal.

Chapter 6—**Anthropological Eyes**

A look at the broader world through anthropological eyes reveals varied attitudes about bodily exposure. Ancient Roman, Egyptian, and Greek civilizations recognized the medicinal properties of the sun, and therefore exposed their full bodies to it as a means of preventive medicine.

Clothing that left a woman's breast exposed was a common style of early Egyptian dress. In Greece, tunics that left one side of the male or female chest exposed were common. Ancient Greek culture was also known for nude sportsmanship. According to Hatton:

> These ancient Greeks, who contributed to Western art the "idealized nude" form, sent their young men to schools called *gymnasiums* (from the root word "*gymnos,*" meaning "naked"), where students exercised and learned their lessons in the nude. Greek athletes stripped themselves entirely bare for all competitive events. Although in Greece this practice of athletic nudity was generally reserved for males, in Sparta, the public practice of naked exercise and competition included young women as well. Most people don't know that the original Greek Olympic games required the full nudity of all competitors.[195]

The prevalence of nudity in Greek sculpture affirms their acceptance of it, and the characteristically small size of the genitalia on male statues reveals a cultural ideal opposite to that of today. In ancient Greece, a small penis was a sign of nobility.[196]

According to Bordo, "Ancient Greece, a highly masculinist culture but also one that placed great emphasis on male self-control in matters of sexuality, favored 'small and taut' genitals." Eva C. Keuls, in her book *The Reign of the Phallus: Sexual Politics in Ancient Athens*, wrote, "Large sex organs were considered coarse and ugly, and were banished to the domains of abstraction, of caricature, of satyrs, and of barbarians."[197]

The Romans, who possessed a more sexualized body consciousness, preferred larger penises. Unlike Greece, they elevated their gods by enlarging their penises when portraying them in art. Rome was also famous for the huge public baths installed in major cities all around the Mediterranean, some of which had the capacity to hold 1,500 people! Fleming, writing for ESPN, pointed out, "In Roman community baths, it was customary for men to stand and applaud when a well-endowed peer entered the water."[198]

In Ancient India, a religious sect known as the Jains featured holy men who walked about nude as a spiritual discipline. They believe it helped them develop independent thought and self-assurance. In his article "Ancient India," Florida State University professor Paul LaValley noted that the Jains practiced nudity "as a method of becoming free from bonds . . . contentment with no clothes."[199]

In tropical cultures such as Sub-Saharan Africa and the Pacific Islands, both male and female nudity is common and often compulsive, with body paint often being all the "covering" needed for adults and children alike.[200]

In modern-day Japanese, Korean, and eastern European cultures, public bathhouses are places for men and women to bathe together, discuss current events, meet friends, and socialize. Genders are separated in areas that require nudity. Examples of such include the sento at the Edo Tokyo Open Air Museum, the Széchenу thermal bath in Budapest, and the Imperial Korean Spa in Fullerton, California (to locate a bathhouse spa in your area, visit saunasplash.com).

Jamie Mackay, an editor at openDemocracy, wrote:

> For most of the history of our species, in most parts of the world, bathing has been a collective act. In ancient Asia, the practice was a religious ritual believed to have

medical benefits related to the purification of the soul and body. For the Greeks, the baths were associated with self-expression, song, dance and sport, while in Rome they served as community centres, places to eat, exercise, read and debate politics.[201]

A Conditioned Response

Aaron Frost, in his book *Christian Body*, wrote about an ancient Persian practice called *purdah,* which requires women to dress in all-enveloping clothes in order to stay out of the sight of men or strangers. "Today we can see purdah most clearly in Islam, but it also has strong influences in Indian culture and Judeo/Christian philosophy. The English language does not have a literal equivalent to the word 'purdah' but our word 'modesty' has been shifted from its original meaning into a concept very much like purdah."[202]

Frost expands on the socializing influence of purdah:

> Decades ago, the Chinese women were known to observe strict rules about keeping the feet from being seen by any man except their husband, but they cared little about exposing the rest of the body. This was a Chinese version of purdah. Early eastern cultures had strict rules for covering the face with masks, but also frequently left the rest of the body uncovered. This was a version of purdah as well. In these cultures where the feet or the face were strictly covered, these parts of the body were sexually objectified, just as we objectify the parts of the body that are most often covered in our own familiar culture . . . In every culture that practices some version of purdah the part of the body they cover becomes dirty and sexualized.[203]

In the Maori tribes of New Zealand, as well as some tribes in Africa, Papua New Guinea, and the Pacific Islands, female breasts are not covered, nor are they sexualized. Rachel Marie Stone, an evangelical Christian who lives in Malawi, wrote:

> Spend any length of time talking to a woman with a baby of nursing age, and you're almost certain to see her take her entire breast out of her shirt and offer it to her baby . . . In a place where the birth rate is high, a single can of formula costs at least two week's [sic] wages, and privacy is hard to come by, nursing in public is pretty much a necessity.[204]

The result of such widespread exposure is that breasts won't turn an eye in Malawi, but according to Stone, ". . . when women wear shorts or skirts above the knee, *everyone*—men, women, even children—has a hard time not staring."[205] A culture in which knees are more sexualized than breasts serves as further evidence that socialization plays a pivotal role in determining our attractions to the body. The wide-eyed arousal of a male exposed to a female chest is a response conditioned by Western standards of dress. *Only what is covered is coveted.*

A mid-nineteenth century edition of *Harper's Bazaar* featured a diagram showing the proper hemline for girls' dresses at various ages. Younger girls could wear skirts as high as the knee, but by the time they reached sixteen years old the dresses had to hang all the way down to the shoe. This contributed significantly to the sexualization of the female leg, which persists in Western culture even today. (You can view this magazine illustration at famousfigleaf.com.)

Frost wrote: "Some people assume we are biologically hard-wired to respond sexually to nudity, but later generations of Pavlov's dogs might as easily assume that all dogs are instinctively hard-wired to drool at the sound of a bell even though that would be false. To assume that nudity causes lust, is like assuming that the bells cause drooling."[206]

Frost grew up in the mud huts of a remote village deep within the Congo, and has traveled extensively through India, Africa, and South America. Having been exposed to a myriad of cultural norms concerning bodily exposure, Frost observed: "In cultures where no part of the body is necessarily covered they have no concept of pornography or sexual objectification of the body."[207]

Hatton, a former maternity nurse, describes how garments preserve an attraction to the body by what they hide. Fig leaves draw both the eye and the mind to what is concealed beneath them:

> When body parts are covered up, it makes you wonder what they would look like uncovered. Your curiosity can run wild. But when the clothing is off, it brings you down to reality. It makes me remember something a teacher told us back in high school. He said a girl on the beach would attract more attention in a bikini than with nothing on. None of us believed him. He said it was because nakedness short-circuits the imagination. That's just what I discovered in my nursing job. The real thing wipes out unreal fantasies.[208]

Frost agrees: "Though it seems counter-intuitive to our backward, legalistic way of thinking, it is actually the clothing that causes the lust, and when those standards are finally removed, the erotic effect quickly disappears . . . The fact is, clothing creates the intrigue that causes temptation."[209]

Stone concludes her article, saying:

> Whatever one thinks of the evangelical modesty movement—and the growing back-and-forth debates online—we must recognize this cultural context for how we perceive what's appropriate. A fixation on our own definition of modesty threatens to warp our perceptions and hurt our interactions with others—particularly as we venture outside our own culture.[210]

In an article written for *Q Ideas,* Rachel Held Evans explains how what is considered modest or appropriate changes depending on culture and context:

> I spent some time in India, where women in traditional saris exposed their midriffs and navels without a second thought, but would carefully avoid showing their knees . . . In many cultures, a one-piece bathing suit would be considered scandalous; in others, bikinis—or even topless bathing—are the norm.[211]

As Nature Intended

A Starbucks in Ottawa, Canada, made the news when one woman scolded another for breastfeeding her crying baby while waiting for a drink refill. Daily Mail Online reported that Julia Wykes said she had no intention of covering her young son while feeding him, because it was over one hundred degrees Fahrenheit that day. Wykes then stated, "I am not going to suffocate my child to save you from the potential glimpse of side-boob."[212]

When the feeding started, one woman loudly complained that it was "disgusting" and ordered the employee behind the counter to "deal with the situation." The barista did no such thing—instead offering the nursing mother a free drink and a heartfelt apology over the situation.

After posting her story on Facebook, Ms. Wykes said some of the comments she received were supportive, but many were abusive. "What shocked me most in all of this is how many of these negative voices came from women. From the original complaining customer to those posting their comments online, I am truly afraid of what it means for our society that adult women find it acceptable to insult and belittle other women for breastfeeding in public—basically for having breasts and using them as nature intended."[213]

This story illustrates how, even in the same country, the same city, *the same coffee shop*, attitudes towards exposure of the body vary substantially.

Incarnational Nudity

In the science fiction novel *Stranger in a Strange Land*, Robert A. Heinlein tells the story of Valentine Michael Smith, a human being raised on Mars. A fresh encounter with Earth creates much confusion, as he struggles to understand the custom and stigma of this new world. When Michaels' nurse Gillian insists that he dress up for an informal gathering, his friend Jubal scolds her for imposing her personal customs on an outsider:

> Here, by the grace of God and an inside straight, we have a personality untouched by the psychotic taboos of our tribe—and you want to turn him into a carbon copy of every fourth-rate conformist in this frightened land! Why don't you go whole hog? Get him a brief case and make him carry it wherever he goes—make him feel shame if he doesn't have it.[214]

These "earthlings" tried to turn Valentine into one of them. Evangelicals taking the gospel to foreign lands have replicated this error. Early missionaries, unable to distinguish human law from God's, used to infect indigenous cultures with their own commercial interests and arbitrary customs, including scrupulous enforcement of Western standards of dress.

In her book *From Jerusalem to Irian Jaya: A Biographical History of Christian Missions*, Ruth Tucker retells Bradford Smith's account of nineteenth-century New Englanders who took the gospel to "savages" on the Hawaiian Islands. "The missionaries had believed they were aiding the cause of morality when they insisted converts wear clothes, 'only to discover,' according to Smith, 'that the clothes the girls put on became a source of allurement to men who all their lives had taken nudity for granted!'"[215]

For Hudson Taylor, taking the gospel to the Chinese wasn't about avoiding the implication of his customs, *but embracing theirs*. When he traded his British knickers for a Mao Suit and queue (Chinese ponytail), his countrymen thought he'd gone mad. To Hudson, exchanging his ruffles for a tunic was synonymous to Christ exchanging his glory for human flesh. For Hudson, incarnational ministry was about what he put on, but to Bishop Alejandro Labaca, a Catholic missionary to the Amazonian Huaorani tribe, incarnational ministry was about what he took off:

> Whenever new missionaries join the group, once again there arise the same worries that arose on our first contacts with the Amazon culture of nakedness. The worry, sometimes bordering on obsession, centers on the fact that the Huaorani strip their visitors naked. Although all of us agreed that nakedness was legal in their culture, this practice was one of the biggest difficulties for the

> entrance of missionary personnel, especially sisters. We very soon came to the conclusion that the missionaries should not wait until they are stripped, but rather anticipate it and do it ourselves in order to show our esteem and appreciation for the culture of the Huaorani people. It should be a sign of our love for the Huaorani and their concrete reality which clashes with our own customs.[216]

By instructing the Corinthians to "endure all things lest we hinder the gospel of Christ,"[217] it was Paul's desire to remove any source of offense excepting the cross itself. Likewise, Bishop Labaca wrote that he "judged that I should conduct myself with complete naturalness, just as they do, accepting everything they do, except sin."[218]

An American Problem

Evangelical missionary groups now understand that the transfer of Western stigma to indigenous standards of dress also imparts the sexualized body consciousness that plagues the Western world. As a result, today's missionaries receive cross-cultural training which precludes them from transferring the morally indifferent customs of their own region, including body taboos.

If missionaries have witnessed, firsthand, the association between the stigmatization of nudity and the sexualization of the body, why have we only revised our methods overseas? Is it possible that, just as Bishop Labaca had a message that would transform the Huaoranis' lives, so too, they had a message that could transform ours?

Hatton recounts, "A pastoral colleague of mine told me about his missionary friend's answer to American visitors who see the nakedness of the native population and ask about 'the nudity problem.' He tells them, 'These people don't have a problem with nudity. It's we Americans who have the problem.'"[219]

In an article written for Alternet.org, Anna Pulley reports on "Five American Sex Norms Europeans Probably Think Are

Insane." Number one on the list is "Extreme violence in the media is fine, just don't show a nipple."[220] Pulley wrote:

> According to reports, the average American child will see 200,000 violent acts and witness 16,000 murders on TV by the time she is 18 . . . While this is considered fine and normal, showing the naked or partially naked human body on TV is considered extremely taboo. When Justin Timberlake accidentally ripped off a piece of Janet Jackson's costume during the Super Bowl halftime show, revealing her nipple for a fraction of a second, this not only caused a moral outrage that lasted for days, but the FCC tried to fine television network CBS $550,000 for broadcasting "indecency."[221]

Pulley concludes:

> A Dutch friend who now lives in London also remarked on this disconnect between violence and nudity: "The movie *Frida* with Salma Hayek is rated R in the U.S. because of nudity, but in Holland it was 6 (for children 6 and older). But many violent movies are 16 in Holland and PG/PG-13 in the U.S. Why are boobs worse than death? How do boobs affect people negatively? Are they scary? Do they make people do bad things? I wanna know!"[222]

George R. R. Martin, author of the *Game of Thrones* series, illustrates this seeming dichotomy between outrage over sex, and violence:

> I can describe an axe entering a human skull in great explicit detail and no one will blink twice at it. I provide a similar description, just as detailed, of a penis entering a vagina, and I get letters about it and people swearing off. To my mind this is kind of frustrating, it's madness. Ultimately, in the history of [the] world, penises entering vaginas have given a lot of people a lot of pleasure; axes entering skulls, well, not so much.[223]

The Gateway Drug to Sex

The physical nature of Christ's ministry shows us that he understood bodily contact was an effective means of demonstrating love. For Christ, the body was the window to the soul. The physical healing which accompanied Jesus' touch further reveals the profound significance he ascribed to the body. Jesus understood that the body, as well as the soul, must be saved. Yet in a culture whose inhabitants are desperate for a hug, Western body taboos have tied the arms of Christ behind his back.

As is the case with nudity, the connotations of physical touch vary widely around the world. In China, it's customary for men to hold hands with men (and women with women) while chatting and walking down the street. The same goes for African countries like Morocco, Botswana, and Sudan, and Middle-Eastern countries like Egypt and Israel. This behavior is also commonplace in Sri Lanka, India, the Philippines, and most of South Asia.

In some of these locales men won't only walk hand in hand, they'll walk arm in arm, or sit on a park bench close enough to be lovers; but they most likely are not. In Ethiopia men express platonic friendship through *gursha*, a friend feeding another friend by hand.

In cultures that haven't sexualized same-gender intimacy, individuals of the same gender can behave like American lovers would in public, yet with no erotic connotation. Taz Liffman wrote:

> There do exist . . . entire countries that look upon two fully-grown heterosexual men holding hands as something perfectly normal. Indeed, as Samir Khalaf, sociology professor at American University of Beirut, explains it, in many cultures the holding of hands is "the warmest expression of affection between men . . . a sign of solidarity and kinship."[224]

According the blog Free Northerner, ". . . there is absolutely nothing implicitly homoerotic about men engaging in physical male bonding. In [the] past, intimate physical contact between men was normal, and in other parts of the world that have not been homoeroticized it still is."[225]

In Western cultures, any form of touch that lasts for more than a few seconds will likely be viewed as an expression of sexual intimacy. This is due, in part, to the traditional Christian teaching on sexuality which, as Lily Dunn puts it, portrays "any and all physical contact" as a "gateway drug to sex."[226]

D. C. McAllister, in her article "How To Stop Sexualizing Everything," wrote that our society needs a "phileo resurgence" to remove sexual connotations from intimate friendship.[227] (*Phileo* is the Greek word used to describe friendship in Scripture.)

McAllister describes an exchange in which her daughter called her "gay" for saying "I love you" to a female friend, and then responds, "I guess I am kind of weird. I confess: I'm very passionate about my friends. But am I the abnormal one, or is there something wrong with our society? My daughter isn't unusual, and her response was pretty typical. Many people have that reaction to women who are passionate about their friends—and even more so for men!"[228]

McAllister blames such attitudes on Puritan influence and Victorian sensibility. "Puritanism put a damper on passions as if they are the seat of evil within the soul . . . This tight control on feelings seeped into our culture, worsened by Victorian aloofness. We became a society that shook hands instead of kissed."[229]

Timmerman wrote about the shift in cultural attitudes about touch that began in the early twentieth century:

> Physical affection was something suspect and not to be trusted. Touch and attitudes about our bodies were questionable at best and seen through a scrim of likely sexual motives. It was an "age of suspicion" where Freud was a key agent. During the sexual revolution of the '60s perhaps we all got back in touch with our bodies and swung to the other end of the Enlightenment's dualism: body good, spirit bad! In some ironic ways we proved the Victorians right as we now view touch, bodies, and most everything through a sexual lens.[230]

America's fear of hugs is another one of Pulleys "Five American Sex Norms Europeans Probably Think Are Insane." She wrote:

> Research has shown that non-sexual physical contact has a profound impact on people's emotional and physical well-being. Despite this knowledge, and our hyper-sexualized tendencies, America is one of the most touch-phobic countries in the world. A global study on touch rated the United States among "the lowest touch countries studied." In contrast, the high-touch countries include Spain, France, Italy, and Greece. Some researchers think our fear of platonic touching actually leads to violence, particularly in young males. In one study, American adolescents were shown to touch each other far less and be more aggressive toward their peers compared with French adolescents.[231]

The level of intimacy permitted in friendship allows most of the world a far more platonic body consciousness than that of the west. Our moral reservations, and fear of exploitation, preclude us from experiencing the kind of corporeal love our bodies crave; and for its lack of tactile affection, society pays a price. Once again, it is not these "other" countries that have a problem; it is we Americans that have the problem.

Chapter 7—**The Naked Cowboy**

Despite varying standards of modesty around the world, some evangelicals still hold that God clothed Adam and Eve to conceal their bodies. But surely the apparel God designed for his beloved had nothing to do with hiding their flesh; from *whom* would it need to be concealed? There's no purpose clothing would serve to hide two bodies from each other in the context of holy matrimony.

When presented with the revelation that something about us is flawed, we instinctively go about the task of trying to hide it from others. When their "eyes were opened," Adam and Eve garnished their genitals with a plant. But that famous fig leaf was only meant to cover their bodies, while God's garment, shaped from the animal sacrificed to atone for mankinds' inaugural sin, was fashioned to cover their souls.

Adam's garment was never meant to conceal his sin, and God's garment was never meant to conceal his body. Indeed it was not God who told his beloved they were naked; it was he who created them as such. The coat of leather was meant only to protect their bodies from the elements, and their souls from his wrath.

From Plants to Pants

Modern apparel has evolved well beyond the fig leaf, yet the notion that righteousness can be achieved by putting on some clothes hasn't changed much since Adam tried it. From plants to pants, clothing is still esteemed as a moral covering. Yet the conflation of dress with modesty is a concept foreign to both the teachings of Christ and the content of the epistles.

Misrepresentation of the Bible's posture on this subject is so widespread it seems perennial, yet this deviation didn't commence until the mid-nineteenth century. Frost asserts that the emergence of Puritan theology during the Victorian era created a shift in Western attitudes toward clothing and nakedness, at which point the Victorian hermeneutic replaced the biblical one.[232] Since that time, biblical teachings about modesty have been warped by biased translators and puritanical preachers.[233]

Frost goes on to explain that "because of this, our Bible translations, commentaries, and church writings express very different perspectives based on whether they come from before or after this pivotal turning point in the history of opinions about the human body."[234]

The King James Version is one example of a "body-friendly" text, as it predates religious modesty standards by several hundred years. Consider the text of Job 31:1 in the post-Victorian New International Version: "I made a covenant with my eyes not to look lustfully at a young woman." The post-Victorian New American Standard Version reads: "I have made a covenant with my eyes; How then could I gaze at a virgin?" Both translations posit the mere act of *looking* as sinful. Now consider the King James Version of this passage:

> I made a covenant with mine eyes; why then should I think upon a maid?

The KJV uses the word *think*, which isn't even a synonym for either of the words used in the aforementioned translations: *look* and *gaze*. The Hebrew word used here is *biyn*, which literally means to "separate mentally." Therefore *think* is a vastly more accurate translation of this word than *look*. The former puts emphasis on what's happening in the mind, while the latter merely refers to where the eyes are pointed.

The difference in meaning between these two words is not trivial, and it is for this reason that I had to use post-Victorian translations for some of the exegesis provided in this book.[235] If I had used the KJV versions, the reader might not even understand why anyone ever thought the passage was prohibiting literal nudity in the first place!

A "Piece of Cake"

In the English language, delicate subjects are often euphemized with figures of speech. According to Frost:

> We are all familiar with the colloquialisms of our own language and culture. "Tie the knot," "deep pockets," "piece of cake" and so on. None of these are literal, so anyone who doesn't speak English fluently or natively may easily be confused or misled by these expressions . . . In English, we all know that when two people "sleep together" they are not sleeping, but if someone found our writings thousands of years from now they might falsely conclude that we thought it was a sin for two people to "sleep together" even though literally being asleep together isn't the issue; it's a euphemism.[236]

The book of Leviticus conveys that, "'If a man takes his sister, his father's daughter or his mother's daughter, and sees her nakedness and she sees his nakedness, it is a wicked thing. And they shall be cut off in the sight of their people. He has uncovered his sister's nakedness. He shall bear his guilt."[237] This passage initially seems to condemn nudity, but the verses that follow provide the context for this instruction:

> You shall not uncover the nakedness of your mother's sister nor of your father's sister, for that would uncover his near of kin. They shall bear their guilt. If a man lies with his uncle's wife, he has uncovered his uncle's nakedness. They shall bear their sin; they shall die childless. If a man takes his brother's wife, it is an unclean thing. He has uncovered his brother's nakedness. They shall be childless.[238]

The law prescribes serious consequences for such an offense, yet the literal translation of the phrase "uncover the nakedness" is to "make naked the(ir) naked(ness)." Similar to the modern-day euphemism of "sleeping together," this is a figure of speech referring to copulation, not exposure. This segment of Scripture is condemning incest, not nudity.

Incest was not initially forbidden by God. It was actually necessary for Adam and Eve's children (and Noah's children) to populate the earth. This Levitical passage marks the beginning of this new prohibition.

The section in between these two, verse 18, also appears to prohibit nudity; but this passage is merely warning that sexual intercourse during a woman's period is unclean:

> If a man lies with a woman during her sickness and uncovers her nakedness, he has exposed her flow, and she has uncovered the flow of her blood. Both of them shall be cut off from their people.[239]

Post-Victorian translations of Job 31:1, Habakkuk 2:15, and Ezekiel 16:36 all contain the same euphemism. Yet in all three instances (and many others), the word translated "nakedness," *'ervah,* is actually referring to some form of sexual impropriety. A different word, *'arowm,* is used for literal nudity in a morally neutral context.

Noah and His Sons

Genesis 9 recounts that Noah got drunk in his tent and "Ham, the father of Canaan, saw the nakedness of his father, and told his two brothers outside."[240] A literal reading of this suggests Ham merely enters the tent, sees his father naked, and then goes out to tell his two brothers. Yet just a couple verses later we read that "Noah awoke from his wine, and knew what his younger son had done to him."[241]

The original word translated "had done to him" is *`asah,* which literally means "to do or make"; so we know that Ham actually *did something* to his father. Since Genesis was written by the same author as Leviticus, we also know that "nakedness" in this passage is a euphemism for some kind of sexual transgression. Scholars have postulated this could have been sodomy, castration, or incest, among others. Scripture doesn't reveal specifically what happened in that tent, but the text clearly demonstrates that Ham's sin wasn't merely "looking" at his father.

Upon hearing of their father's nakedness, Ham's brothers approached their father from behind carrying a blanket on their shoulders and "went backward and covered the nakedness [*'ervah*] of their father. Their faces were turned away, and they did not see their father's nakedness."[242]

Ezekiel paints a picture of God entering into covenant with Israel by asserting that he "spread the corner of my garment over you and covered your naked body. I gave you my solemn oath and entered into a covenant with you, declares the Sovereign LORD."[243] Just as in Genesis 9, *'ervah* is the word used for "nakedness" in this text. Yet in this case the word refers to the shame of Israel's transgressions. Rather than dole out his wrath, God chooses to overlook the sin of his beloved, opting to cover her nakedness with his mercy.

Just as God chose to cover up the shame of Israel as an act of mercy, so too did Shem and Japheth cover up the shame of their father. They weren't approaching Noah from behind to avoid seeing his body exposed; *they were doing it to avoid seeing his indignity exposed.* Ham's brothers behaved as they did as an act of respect, to spare their father from any further humiliation.

Biblical Modesty

Across the globe there are vastly varying concepts of what is proper when it comes to bodily exposure, and each culture assumes their own standards of dress are ubiquitous. Frost points out that "these subconscious ideas influence the way we perceive things, and they invariably color the way we understand the Bible."[244]

Hatton expands on this idea, pointing out that the biblical definition of modesty has been contaminated by the biased assumptions of contemporary culture:

> The modern idea of modesty, focused on hiding body parts, subverts the intent of Biblical writers, whose definition of modesty had nothing to do with bodily exposure. For Paul and Peter, modesty was godly humility adorned with holy virtues. Even as late as 1828, Webster's definition of the word "modesty" still included nothing about dress.[245]

Hatton goes on to explain that nowhere in Scripture is nakedness, by itself, portrayed as scandalous:

> Throughout the Bible, unless it alludes to or is the result of coercion, religious disrespect, sexual misconduct, or physical or spiritual poverty, nakedness by itself is never portrayed as a shameful or immoral condition. Unless it is motivated by impure desires, seeing nakedness is not a shameful or immoral action.[246]

In 1 Timothy 2:9–10 the Apostle Paul instructs: "that the women adorn themselves in modest apparel, with propriety and moderation, not with braided hair or gold or pearls or costly clothing, but, which is proper for women professing godliness, with good works."[247]

In New Testament times, the word translated *modesty* didn't refer to bodily exposure in any sense (revealing attire would not have been titillating as nudity was commonplace in ancient Palestine); rather, it referred to *conduct*. While Paul's definition of conduct did involve clothing, it wasn't the lack of it that he was prohibiting; quite the contrary, it was the excess.

The Greek word used for *modesty* in this passage is *kosmios*, which refers generally to a person's arrangement or composure, signifying that Paul's admonition here is one towards humility of character and simplicity of apparel. Evans provides further insight on the meaning of this word:

> Derived from kosmos (the universe), it signifies orderliness, self-control and appropriateness. It appears only twice in the New Testament, and interestingly, its second usage refers specifically to men (1 Timothy 3:2). In fact, nearly all of the Bible's instructions regarding modest clothing refer not to sexuality, but rather materialism (Isaiah 3:16–23, 1 Timothy 2:9–12, 1 Peter 3:3). Writers in both the Old Testament and New Testament express grave concern when the people of God flaunt their wealth by buying expensive clothes and jewelry while many of their neighbors suffered in poverty.[248]

Frost explains: "Paul's word for 'modesty' is a prohibition of fancy ostentation and opulence in all areas of life . . . Wherever we go we should seek to dress in a way that would downplay any facade of status, elitism, or wealth that would draw attention to self-superiority."[249]

Matthew Henry, in his commentary on the Bible, wrote: "Good works are the best ornament; these are, in the sight of God, of great price. Those that profess godliness should, in their dress, as well as other things, act as becomes their profession; instead of laying out their money on fine clothes, they must lay it out in works of piety and charity, which are properly called good works."[250]

Biblical modesty had more to do with avoiding materialism and stewarding one's time (minutes spent primping oneself in the mirror can be put to better use serving the poor), than with arousing sexuality. It should also be noted that Paul's reference to modesty appears in the context of his giving instruction on worship in a church setting, not in an admonition towards sexual purity.

In his role as a maternity nurse, Hatton recounts a common conversation he's had with women preparing to disrobe: "I often correct patients who say 'I guess this is where I lose my modesty.' I tell them, 'Not at all! You're as modest as the day you were born.'"[251]

The attempt to divorce modesty's definition from the context of nudity is a controversial one, especially against the backdrop of Western civilization's hypersexualized body consciousness. Notwithstanding, it cannot, and should not, be ignored that Scripture reveals a vastly different ethos of bodily exposure than what modern-day evangelicalism has embraced.

In his book *Earthen Vessels*, Matthew Lee Anderson wrote:

> From what I can tell, when evangelicals talk about the body, we say all the right things—but we simply have not thought about the body enough to ensure that our account of its goodness takes its cues from Scripture rather than the broken world around us.[252]

An Innocent Lamb

The story of David and Bathsheba is often referenced as a biblical admonition of nudity, as if Bathsheba was tempting David by bathing in the courtyard. Yet every other woman in Jerusalem did the same thing. Whether male or female, rich or poor, outdoor bathing was universal to the ancient cultures of both Egypt and Israel. The second chapter of Exodus even recounts Pharaoh's daughter bathing in the open river while Jewish commoners walk about.[253]

Women participating in the culturally natural phenomenon of open bathing was not anything King David wasn't used to seeing on a daily basis. What led him to rape his neighbor's wife was not her public bath, but the evil in his own heart. Furthermore, if Bathsheba had committed any sin by exposing her body in public, it would seem odd that Nathan made her the "innocent lamb" in his story.[254]

In both Old and New Testament times, it was common not only to bathe, but also to work in the nude. Prior to the advent of the sewing machine, garments had to be woven by hand—a lengthy and expensive process involving treating, dying, spinning, and weaving. In Bible times, most people could only afford a single garment, usually a simple robe or a tunic.

> If you lend money to any of My people who are poor among you, you shall not be like a moneylender to him; you shall not charge him interest. If you ever take your neighbor's garment as a pledge, you shall return it to

> him before the sun goes down. For that is his only covering, it is his garment for his skin. What will he sleep in? And it will be that when he cries to Me, I will hear, for I am gracious.[255]

As this passage illustrates, anyone whose lone garment was lost or stolen went naked. Such loss brought the shame of poverty, not of exposure. The cultural conflation of wealth with spirituality caused many to assume those who had no clothes were frowned upon by God. Frost wrote: "People were not ashamed to be naked; they were ashamed to be poor."[256]

The Naked Gardener

Individuals couldn't afford to soil their only drape during manual labor, or they'd have nothing to wear in town while it sun-dried from its subsequent wash. Sweat and frequent washing wore out even the best linens rapidly.

Despite the cultural norm of working in the buff, nudity in formal settings was still shameful and embarrassing; the modern-day equivalent of showing up to a dinner party in a bathing suit. It was for these reasons that those few who were wealthy enough to afford two garments, were instructed by John to give the surplus away:

> He answered and said to them, "He who has two tunics, let him give to him who has none; and he who has food, let him do likewise."[257]

Indeed, Jesus wasn't being metaphoric when he said "I was naked and you clothed me . . ."[258] He was speaking of a truly naked person who lacked the warmth and status of a garment. Consider the words of Jesus when warning of the coming desolation, "And let him who is in the field not go back to get his clothes."[259]

Common people simply couldn't afford to work in their clothes, and Peter was no exception:

> Therefore that disciple whom Jesus loved saith unto Peter, It is the Lord. Now when Simon Peter heard that it

> was the Lord, he girt his fisher's coat unto him, (for he was naked,) and did cast himself into the sea.[260]

Having left his linens inside the tomb, Jesus appeared to Mary Magdalene following his resurrection; yet Mary thinks nothing of being approached by a completely naked stranger except to assume he was the gardener:

> Then the disciples went away again to their own homes. But Mary stood outside by the tomb weeping, and as she wept she stooped down and looked into the tomb. And she saw two angels in white sitting, one at the head and the other at the feet, where the body of Jesus had lain. Then they said to her, "Woman, why are you weeping?" She said to them, "Because they have taken away my Lord, and I do not know where they have laid Him." Now when she had said this, she turned around and saw Jesus standing there, and did not know that it was Jesus. Jesus said to her, "Woman, why are you weeping? Whom are you seeking?" She, *supposing Him to be the gardener*, said to Him, "Sir, if You have carried Him away, tell me where You have laid Him, and I will take Him away." Jesus said to her, "Mary!" She turned and said to Him, "Rabboni!" (which is to say, Teacher).[261]

Undignified

A well-known worship song, which is based on a passage in 2 Samuel, proclaims: "I'll become even more undignified than this, some may say its foolishness. But I'll become even more undignified than this."[262] The song goes on to celebrate the act of dancing before the Lord, but David wasn't undignified in this passage merely because he was dancing wildly. He was undignified because he was completely naked from the waist down:

> Then David danced before the Lord with all his might; and David was wearing a linen ephod. So David and all the house of Israel brought up the ark of the Lord with shouting and with the sound of the trumpet. Now as

> the ark of the Lord came into the City of David, Michal, Saul's daughter, looked through a window and saw King David leaping and whirling before the Lord; and she despised him in her heart." . . . Then David returned to bless his household. And Michal the daughter of Saul came out to meet David, and said, "How glorious was the king of Israel today, uncovering himself today in the eyes of the maids of his servants, as one of the base fellows shamelessly uncovers himself!" So David said to Michal, "It was before the Lord, who chose me instead of your father and all his house, to appoint me ruler over the people of the Lord, over Israel. Therefore I will play music before the Lord. And I will be even more undignified than this, and will be humble in my own sight. But as for the maidservants of whom you have spoken, by them I will be held in honor."[263]

David's only covering, an ephod, was a small vest usually worn by priests over their other garments. Michal believed David had disgraced himself by exposing his body to the slave girls. David was fast to clarify, he wasn't dancing naked for them, *he was doing it for the Lord.*

The Naked Prophets

In foretelling the destruction of Samaria and Jerusalem, so grieved is Micah by the conduct of God's people that he asserts: "Therefore I will wail and howl, I will go stripped and naked; I will make a wailing like the jackals And a mourning like the ostriches . . ."[264] Even King Saul "stripped off his clothes and prophesied before Samuel in like manner, and lay down naked all that day and all that night. Therefore they say, 'Is Saul also among the prophets?'"[265]

Some scholars insist that Saul wasn't completely naked, claiming that he only removed his cloak, not his tunic. But the Hebrew word for *naked* in this passage is *'arowm*, which is the same word used in Genesis to describe Adam and Eve before the fall.[266] Had Saul been only partially nude, there is a word Samuel could have used for that: *galah*. It's the same word Samuel used to describe David's state of dancing before the Lord wearing only an ephod.

Before raising Lazarus, Jesus specifically ordered his grave clothes removed. Hatton observes, "Without those wrappings, his body's only covering was the joyous embrace of his two sisters."[267] Fully unclothed, Lazarus proceeded to greet and talk with the surrounding mourners and relatives until someone brought his robe from inside the house.

The body of Dorcas hadn't even been wrapped yet when, following Peter's prayer, she sprung to life. So overjoyed was Peter, that he didn't even retrieve her garment before calling the grieving saints back into the room. Ironically, Dorcas was a seamstress that had made the very garments worn by many of those in the room, yet the joy of the moment seemed to eclipse her need for clothing.[268]

Perhaps it was this same joy that caused onlookers to carpet Christ's path into Jerusalem with the clothes off their own bodies:

> And a very great multitude spread their clothes on the road; others cut down branches from the trees and spread them on the road.[269]

Translators or Tailors?

Jesus told his disciples, "If anyone wants to sue you and take away your tunic, let him have your cloak also."[270] The words *cloak* and *tunic* are referring to the inner and outer garments. A cloak is a long garment worn over the shoulders that is sometimes hooded; basically a cape. A tunic is a garment worn over the torso, with or without sleeves, and of various lengths reaching from the hips to the ankles.

When reading this passage it's important to understand that the concept we know as "pants" didn't exist in ancient Palestine. So Jesus' command to give up both the cloak and tunic was essentially a command to strip naked. According to Frost:

> When Jesus specifically states that *both* the cloak *and* the tunic should be given away, He is very clearly talking about making a complete sacrifice to the point where you were left to continue on your way completely naked (as the other person had been moments before). What Jesus teaches here is a level of self-sacrifice where we do not merely divide our belongings evenly, but generously trade places entirely with someone who is too poor to own clothing and instead go completely naked ourselves.[271]

Modern translators often assumed that anyone who removed an item of clothing had a layer left, even if there's nothing in the original text to support it. This is a hasty assumption, since not everyone had the means to own two garments; as Jesus pointed out, *many didn't even have the means to own one.*

For example, in the "body-friendly" KJV, the Apostle John's description of Peter fishing in the nude reads: "Therefore that disciple whom Jesus loved saith unto Peter, It is the Lord. Now when Simon Peter heard that it was the Lord, he girt his fisher's coat unto him, (for he was naked,) and did cast himself into the sea."[272]

The post-Victorian NASB removed the word *naked* and replaced it with something entirely different:

> Therefore that disciple whom Jesus loved said to Peter, "It is the Lord." So when Simon Peter heard that it was the Lord, he put his *outer garment* on (for he was stripped for work), and threw himself into the sea.[273]

The word *outer* does not appear in any of the original Greek manuscripts, nor is it even implied. Therefore, in this instance, the word was not translated from any other word; it was simply *added* to the text. Furthermore, stone reliefs and mosaics from this era clearly depict sailors, fisherman, and other laborers working stark naked.

This isn't the only place in Scripture where translators have added clothing to a passage that contains no language whatsoever to indicate it was ever there. The translators have dressed so many of the prophets and apostles, one might start to wonder if their function is more akin to a tailor than a translator.

Consider Ruth, the impoverished widow, who had been gleaning grain in the fields of Boaz. As was common to agrarian society, Ruth was working in the nude; but when she wanted to approach Boaz with a request, her mother-in-law replied: "Wash yourself therefore, and anoint yourself and put on your *best* clothes, and go down to the threshing floor; but do not make yourself known to the man until he has finished eating and drinking."[274]

It seems like translators of the NASB added the word *best* to create the impression that Ruth was already wearing clothes, and just needed to change into something "nicer." Just as in the previous example, this translation is not justified by any elements from the original text; the word was merely added. Remove the fabricated adjective, and the text reads: "put on your clothes, and go down to the threshing floor."

Yet another example of this contrivance is found in Luke 17:7–8, for which the NASB reads: "Which of you, having a slave plowing or tending sheep, will say to him when he has come in from the field, 'Come immediately and sit down to eat'? But will he not say to him, 'Prepare something for me to eat, and *properly* clothe yourself and serve me while I eat and drink; and afterward you may eat and drink'?"[275]

The KJV simply reads "gird yourself," which literally translates to "clothe yourself." The NASB adds the word *properly* to imply Luke is suggesting one should merely change clothes, rather than transition from a state of complete undress.

John 13:3–5 reads: "Jesus . . . rose from supper and laid aside His garments, took a towel and girded Himself. After that, He poured water into a basin and began to wash the disciples' feet, and to wipe them with the towel with which He was girded."[276]

Frost wrote:

> For several years I have wondered how Jesus might have washed His disciples' feet with a towel that was wrapped around His waist. I remember puzzling about that even as a child. It just seems like an awkward and difficult maneuver to perform. Upon looking into the text, the word translated as "girded" in the English is not the

> word for putting on clothing that would be worn as a garment. The standard Greek word for "gird" or "put on" clothing literally means "to wrap around" in Greek, but this verse uses a different verb which definitely points out that Jesus did *not* wrap the towel around His waist. Instead, a different word is used to describe what He did with the towel. It is a less common word without a clearly known meaning, but it seems Jesus "slung" it over His shoulder or forearm as a naked slave would normally do while washing feet.[277]

Baptism in the Buff

The normalcy of nudity in Israel might explain why Isaiah wasn't petrified when God commanded him to go about preaching his message naked and barefoot for three years.

At one point during Hatton's fictional walk in the woods he is transported back in time, encountering a group reminiscent of first-century Gentile Christians dressed in ancient garb and speaking koine Greek. They are baptizing each other in the nude. Awestruck at first, Hatton soon realizes this was the ritual norm in the Roman Empire during the time of Christ.

Soon thereafter Hatton is spotted by the group's leader, an ancient minister, who engages Hatton in a discourse on the normalcy of nudity in his own era:

> Yes, you read it often . . . how God commanded Isaiah to go about preaching God's message barefoot and naked for three years . . . You already know the public outcry you would face today for obeying such a command. But in Isaiah's village, his obedience to God troubled no one. None of his neighbors were offended by naked preaching. Why would they be? A naked preacher was no strange sight to them, whether it be Isaiah or Micah or some other prophet. Those who watched King Saul prophesying naked all night under the stars also took him to be "*among the prophets*."[278]

The venerable preacher goes on to say that, while prophets were usually seen unclad only for practical reasons (such as working in a garden or bathing in the river), Isaiah's naked message "turned him into a living parable of his own task to unveil the truth,"[279] thereby affirming the transparency of his message. Isaiah's literal nudity was a spiritual metaphor, just like the ritual *mikveh,* the Jewish precursor for what Christ would one day ordain as baptism. The preacher continued:

> In his preaching, John proclaimed this baptism as a sign of repentance. After our Lord's resurrection, the Holy Spirit gave it even deeper meaning. But both John's practice and ours followed the Jewish custom of removing all clothing. To the Jews, it represented a return to the innocence of Adam and Eve, but to us it signified a purifying death. By taking off our clothes we symbolically stripped ourselves from the clinging habits of worldliness, removing the rags of our own righteousness. Our nakedness displayed our confidence in being washed completely in Christ's blood and our need to be buried with Him in death. We rose from the water fully cleansed, entering a new way of life, even as naked newborns leave the womb to enter a new world . . . Baptism has forever been a full and true bath, intended to wash the whole body with water, even as the Spirit washes the entire soul with the Word.[280]

Given that outdoor bathing was already normal practice in most ancient civilizations, nude baptism was not regarded as indecent. In fact, this is likely the mode of baptism used by John the Baptist, since it had already been recognized by the Jews. And consider the words of the early church father Cyril of Jerusalem:

> You put off your clothes, which is an emblem of putting off the old man with his deeds; and being thus divested, you stood naked, imitating Christ, that was naked upon the cross, who by his nakedness spoiled principalities and powers, publicly triumphing over them in the cross.[281]

Another church father, Theodore of Mopsuestia, wrote:

> Adam was naked at the beginning, and unashamed. This is why your clothing must be taken off as baptism restores right relation to God.[282]

While listening to the preacher from antiquity expound on these very things, Hatton finds himself re-imagining the descent of the Holy Spirit, in the context of his fresh epiphany: "*What would it have looked like? . . . Downtown Jerusalem on the Day of Pentecost, and a few thousand people getting baptized nude!*"[283]

The Naked Cowboy

Fast forward to 2016, at a Hillsong Church women's conference in New York City, where one of the pastors playfully sang a song wearing nothing but a pair of square-cut shorts, a cowboy hat, and his guitar. He was trying to portray one of the city's famous street performers known as "The Naked Cowboy." The guy wasn't really naked, but evangelicals still went berserk.

Christian author Joe Dallas wrote on his Facebook page "when self-identified believers wallow in apostate behavior while the church ladies cheer them on, then who needs Satan?"[284] (Joe is a man for whom I have tremendous respect; but on this particular subject we disagree.)

Dallas' post was subsequently flooded with indignant churchgoers criticizing this church for its "worldliness," and condemning Hillsong's pastor for being a "stumbling block." One commenter went as far as to write, "Hillsong needs to stop calling themselves a church. They are not, they are just a strip club."[285]

Has modern evangelicalism so profoundly sexualized its body consciousness that a male cannot even expose his chest at church without being dubbed apostate?

The Weaker Brother

The Apostle Paul instructs the Romans not to put a "stumbling block or a cause to fall in our brother's way."[286] And again to the Corinthians Paul instructs:

> But beware lest somehow this liberty of yours become a stumbling block to those who are weak. For if anyone sees you who have knowledge eating in an idol's temple, will not the conscience of him who is weak be emboldened to eat those things offered to idols? And because of your knowledge shall the weak brother perish, for whom Christ died? But when you thus sin against the brethren, and wound their weak conscience, you sin against Christ.[287]

Loren Seibold, in his article "The Tyranny of the Weaker Brother," wrote "The weaker brother must be weak in faith, not simply opinionated or dictatorial."[288]

Seibold explains that if parishioners oblige the weaker brother, it is not because he is right, but because he is weak. "Paul urges accommodation of the weak only in a certain situation: when someone is pushed unnecessarily beyond the stage of growth he has achieved, and then only in matters where all that is at stake is a small self-abridgment of one's own freedom until the weaker ones can mature."[289]

The application of Paul's instruction outside of its proper context subjects a church body to the tyranny of the one who demands all conform to his convictions, lest he "stumble." But giving in to such demands serves only to prolong the adolescence of the weaker believer. Seibold asserts:

> When an infant is learning to walk, you clear a path so his little feet will not stumble, and hold out your hands to catch him should he fall. You would not, for the rest of her life, clear every path and hold out your hands for her to walk into. You want him to learn to climb stairs, to hike over rough ground, to play games without tripping over his or someone else's feet . . . It's hard to see how Paul, who never tolerated a Judaizer's religion, would have intended that we should simply yield to

> those weaker brothers or sisters who demand their way rather than encouraging them to mature in their relationship with Christ.[290]

Additionally, many hold that Paul's Thessalonian command to abstain from the "appearance of evil"[291] prohibits Christian behavior that could merely be *perceived* as unholy. Such interpretation holds our every action in bondage to the subjective perceptions of others.

After healing a man on the Sabbath, Jesus chastised the Jews for doing that very thing when he said "Do not judge according to appearance, but judge with righteous judgment."[292] The Greek word for appearance in this verse is *opsis*, which means "the outward appearance, look."[293] Yet the Greek word for *appearance* in 1 Thessalonians 5:22 is *eidos*, which refers not to superficial appearance, but actual manifestation. In fact the same word is translated "shape" in both Luke 3:22 and John 5:37. *Eidos* is not referring to the mere likeness of evil, but to the actual materialization of it. For this reason most modern translations have replaced "appearance of evil" with "every kind of evil" or "every form of evil."

If appearance alone is worthy of rebuke, then Christ himself would come under judgment for permitting such thorough, and intimate, touch from a woman "who was a sinner" (most scholars assume her to have been a prostitute). It was a scandal that Christ permitted a woman touch him at all, let alone allowing her to kiss his bare feet, and caress them with her hair:

> Then one of the Pharisees asked Him to eat with him. And He went to the Pharisee's house, and sat down to eat. And behold, a woman in the city who was a sinner, when she knew that Jesus sat at the table in the Pharisee's house, brought an alabaster flask of fragrant oil, and stood at His feet behind Him weeping; and she began to wash His feet with her tears, and wiped them with the hair of her head; and she kissed His feet and anointed them with the fragrant oil.[294]

In a culture where sexual identity is drenched in uncertainty, one cannot possibly ascertain, from mere appearance, whether one has subjected themself to temptation. The boys-like-girls paradigm of sexual orientation, and male/female polarity of gender that marked yesteryear, has been replaced with a buffet of dysphorias, desires, and designations. (There are now, seemingly, as many different sexual orientations as there are Christian denominations.)

Evangelicals instantly presumed vain imaginations of the women who sang along to the Naked Cowboy's song, yet, without seeing inside their hearts, such judgments can only consist of assumption and conjecture. It is here that our Christian standard of modesty doubles, esteeming the body as both a holy temple and lustful enticement in the same breath.

Indeed there is a context for both; but when the lines are drawn by the subjective judgments of fallible people, instead of a Holy God who sees our true motives, there's no context for nudity outside of a doctor visit or shower that won't arouse religious suspicions of impropriety.

A male who exhibits his flesh for erotic titillation posits the body as the cause of unholy thought, and source of defilement; yet Jesus professed that what defiles us *comes from within.*[295]

Nothing that God created is the source of our human temptation. To the contrary! The human body is the crown of God's creation—consummated by his declaration that *it was good*. That God's people are unable to view the body without sinning is not an indictment of the body itself, but of the immaturity of the postmodern evangelical mind.

One cannot blame their sin on the object of their sin. As St. Augustine so aptly phrased it, "greed . . . is not something wrong with gold."[296]

A Wave of Guilt

The tyranny of the weak has also been used to shame, control, and manipulate females to scrupulous standards of dress; effectively holding women accountable for the thoughts of men. Rather than telling the women of Jerusalem to dress more modestly,

Jesus instructed his male disciples to gouge their eyes out if they used them to lust.

Evans points out that, by this declaration, Jesus took the position opposite of traditional Christians: placing the responsibility for lust on the person doing the lusting, not the other way around.

While growing up, Evans tried "desperately to cover up the shape"[297] of her breasts to avoid the "wave of guilt"[298] that would rush over her if she caught a male classmate checking her out. Evans wrote, "if the female form is treated as inherently seductive and problematic, then women will inevitably feel ashamed of their bodies."[299] Evans goes on to describe the dichotomy of expectations that exists between Christian culture and secular society:

> On the one hand, we are all familiar with the dreaded walk down the grocery store checkout aisle, where magazine after magazine boasts airbrushed photos of impossibly thin celebrities and headlines promising to teach us how to "please our men" with sexier bodies, more fashionable clothes, hotter sex moves and better flirtation skills. Ours is indeed a culture that tends to assign value to a woman based on her sex appeal rather than her character, and that's something we must work to change. But many of us are also familiar with the other extreme. We know what it feels like to have rulers slapped against our bare legs so our Sunday school teachers can measure the length of our skirts. We know how hard it is to do a cannonball into a swimming pool when you're wearing a giant "Jesus Saves" T-shirt over your bathing suit . . . While popular culture tends to disempower women by telling them they must dress to get men to look at them, the modesty culture tends to disempower women by telling them they must dress to keep men from looking at them. In both cases, the impetus is placed on the woman to accommodate her clothing or her body to the (varied and culturally relative) expectations of men. In both cases, it becomes the woman's job to manage the sexual desires of men . . .[300]

Consistent with her belief that women are not responsible for the thoughts of men, Evans asserts that women select clothing to accommodate their own comfort and style, regardless of its impact on others: "Don't dress for men; dress for yourself."[301]

Jessica Rey, who founded a company that designs modest swimsuits for women, asserts, "Modesty isn't about covering up our bodies because they're bad. Modesty isn't about hiding ourselves; it's about revealing our dignity."[302] Rey also wrote a book called *Decent Exposure*, in which she sought to teach women how to "live decently in an indecently exposed world."[303]

Reys' endeavor to provide swimwear for women who want more covering is noble. At the same time Evans is right that we should not dress for others. Just as David dressed not to appease Michal but "unto the Lord," we should dress not to placate the perceptions of others, but towards the expression of our personality and the satisfaction of our spirits.

In fact, the equation of conservative dress with modesty actually creates a false illusion that prevents personal introspection. With clothes on we count ourselves modest; without them we are immodest. This protocol allows us to believe ourselves modest simply by pulling on a thick sweater or stepping into a pair of loose slacks, but never asks us to gauge the condition of our true hearts. C. S. Lewis wrote, "Yet could it be possible, in the long run, to wear clothes without learning modesty, and through modesty lasciviousness?"[304]

Ultimately, the standard isn't whether our apparel causes another to objectify our body, but whether it causes *us* to. If our attire is revealing, is the motive to achieve comfort, express personality, or is it to draw an unholy gaze? Do the clothes in our wardrobe cause us to esteem ours bodies as objects of honor, or of lust? These questions help us gauge the heart, and intentions, of the only person whose thoughts we are actually responsible for: *ours*.

Chapter 8—**Born Again Bodies**

From the time we start grade school, the cruel mechanism of Western socialization directs us to esteem our embodiment based on a very narrow range of acceptable body types. For men, the quintessential "V" shape resulting from slim hips and a muscular chest; and for women, the consummate hourglass figure prototypical of twenty-first century vogue. Both must exhibit facial symmetry and unblemished skin.

Casey Rock, a Christian yoga instructor, wrote, "Our bodies are denounced on the playground."[305] She goes on to say that our peers serve as "a host of examiners more exacting than any pageant panel" pointing out every flaw, blemish, and defect.[306] (If all this is happening with clothes *on*, it's no wonder these kids don't want to shower together when they reach junior high.)

But it wasn't always like this. Sarah Grogan, in her book *Body Image*, wrote:

> Within Western industrialized cultures, there have been many changes over the years in the body shape and size that is considered attractive and healthy, especially for women. It is possible to trace a cultural change in the ideal body from the voluptuous figures favored from the Middle Ages to the turn of the twentieth century, to the thin body types favored by the fashion magazines of today.[307]

Vessels for Consumption

In paintings, the medieval equivalent of modern fashion magazines, the "reproductive figure" was idealized by artists; replete with a plump rounded stomach, hips, and breasts. A sign of fertility, this look characterized the aesthetic ideal of its time.

Glorification of the robust figure endured for another five centuries, even as motivations for its repute shifted. For example, in the early 1900s the slender form was associated with sickness due to the plague of tuberculosis in the United States and Britain.

Up until 1920 clothing styles were portrayed by hand-drawn illustrations, at which time they were replaced by photographs of real people. Body scholars posit this as the decade that slim became the ideal and, to the bewilderment of no one, 1920 was also the year eating disorders became recognized as a formidable malady.[308]

In the years that followed, but particularly from the 1960s to the 1980s, the ideal shape for a woman became slimmer and slimmer. Waists got thinner, models got taller, and boobs got bigger. Cosmetic surgery, dieting, exercise, weight lifting, and steroid use were all tools to help both men and women emphasize the parts they liked and reduce those they didn't.

It brings to mind how factory farms pump chickens full of growth-promoting antibiotics to increase the size of meatier portions, leaving the rest of the body frail and anemic. It's all consistent with a social climate that views bodies, of both humans and animals, as nothing more than vessels for consumption—pronouncing the parts we enjoy, while minimizing those we don't.

Mythical Standards

Body dissatisfaction among Westerners parallels consumption of our media, which digitally brushes, filters, and tones bodies to accomplish a standard of beauty that's impossible for any real person to achieve. Creating an archetype that is unattainable infinitely secures consumer demand for the products that promise to make it so.

The "Daedalic" style popularized in the seventh century BC, which portrayed females as flatly geometric with a high waist and formless drapery, was an ideal modeled after the Greek sculptor

Daedalus. He was literally a mythical character, making him just as "real" as the airbrushed models in twenty-first-century fashion magazines.

Research suggests that as Western media has spread across other cultures, so has body dissatisfaction. Grogan wrote:

> Some authors have suggested that Western media are responsible for the development of body dissatisfaction and eating problems in cultures where such concerns had previously been rare. In a study reporting data from semistructured interviews with adolescent women in a rural community in western Fiji three years after Western television became available, Becker (2004) has shown that women reported explicit modeling of Western media models. They also reported developing weight and shape preoccupation, and purging behavior to control weight. A similar pattern of results was found by Lauren Williams *et al.* (2006) in interviews with 16 Fijian and European Australian 13–18-year-old girls. They found that both groups of girls experienced body concerns including body dissatisfaction and a preference for thinness.[309]

Furthermore, according to Grogan, "Research in South America (Negrao and Cordas, 1996), South Korea (Kim and Kim, 2001), and Japan (Nagami, 1997) has indicated that in cultures where extreme thinness previously signified disease and poverty, many women now aspire to the thin Western body shape ideal."[310]

The irony of this research is that fast food, now a worldwide phenomenon, is a purely American invention. The United States not only exports the desire to be slender, it also perpetuates the diet that makes it an impossibility.

Fat Chance

It's easy to assume that the primary victims of media messages that perpetuate body ideals are those who don't fit them. But with only a few exceptions, the mythical archetype has us *all* feeling flawed.

Even the slender constantly assert that they "feel" fat, indicating that, for some, this dreaded adjective has far more to do with a person's self-perception than their actual size.

Susan Bordo wrote:

> It's a depressingly well-documented fact that when girls and women are asked to draw their bodies or indicate their body size with their hands, they almost always overestimate how much space they take up, and tend to see themselves as too fat no matter how thin they are. This once was thought to be a "body image distortion" unique to those with anorexia nervosa. We now know that seeing oneself as "too fat" is a norm of female perception. Statistics on average weights and medical charts are irrelevant. What matters is the gap between the self and the cultural images. We measure ourselves not against an ideal of health, not even usually (although sometimes) against each other, but against created icon's, fantasies made flesh. Flesh *designed* to arouse admiration, envy, desire.[311]

The real tragedy of Western body ideals is the subtext that's assigned to individuals based solely on their shape. Research has found that a slender, toned body is associated with being in control of one's life: happiness, success, youth. The overweight are often viewed as being less active, intelligent, and social; however they are also seen as warmer and friendlier, consistent with the stereotype of the "fat and jolly" person (e.g., Santa Claus).[312] Grogan summarizes, "the outward appearance of the body is seen as a symbol of personal order or disorder."[313]

Black subculture, in which excess weight is sometimes viewed as desirable, might be an exception to this phenomenon, along with cultures that place less emphasis on independence and individual responsibility. Grogan wrote, "If overweight is seen as being caused by factors within the individual's control (through overeating and lack of exercise), then overweight people are more likely to be stigmatized."[314]

Grogan cites a study that found students in Mexico, whose culture places more emphasis on cultural than personal influences, were less likely to view weight as being within a person's control, and therefore less likely to stigmatize the obese.[315] She wrote "[This study] stresses that prejudice against overweight is culturally bound and depends on attribution of blame."[316]

The Last Bastion of Bigotry

In a 2010 op ed in the *Washington Post*, Deborah L. Rhode cites numerous examples of the overweight and "ugly" being discriminated against. Better looking people are more likely to be hired, get promoted, and even make more money than those that society considers unattractive. Physically attractive people also get higher grades and better justice in the court system. Rhode reported:

> When researchers ask people to evaluate written essays, the same material receives lower ratings for ideas, style and creativity when an accompanying photograph shows a less attractive author . . . Not even justice is blind. In studies that simulate legal proceedings, unattractive plaintiffs receive lower damage awards. And in a study released this month, Stephen Ceci and Justin Gunnell, two researchers at Cornell University, gave students case studies involving real criminal defendants and asked them to come to a verdict and a punishment for each. The students gave unattractive defendants prison sentences that were, on average, 22 months longer than those they gave to attractive defendants.[317]

Rhode concludes that "looks are the last bastion of acceptable bigotry."[318]

To the churchgoer, the judging, stereotyping, and blaming of the obese and "unattractive" is a crime that's easy to deflect onto secular society. Yet despite what few sermons might have been preached against the sin of vanity, traditional Christianity has done our part in perpetuating these societal ideals.

Born Again Bodies

In 1957 Presbyterian minister Charlie Shedd released the book *Pray Your Weight Away*. Shedd condemned obesity as an outward manifestation of inner transgression. Since then, the Christian fitness culture has become a multi-million dollar industry.

Books like *Slim for Him*, *The Hallelujah Diet*, *Body by God*, *Fit for God*, and *What Would Jesus Eat* seek to apply biblical principles to corporeal lifestyle practices. It's a worthwhile task, to be sure; even this author believes that to care for the body is to care for the soul. Unfortunately this truth has been muddied by those who seek to equate a person's physical appearance with their spiritual holiness. R. Marie Griffith, author of the book *Born Again Bodies*, wrote, "While repeatedly decrying the material rewards of slenderness offered by the secular world as superficial, these Christian writers appeal to them constantly."[319]

One author wrote, "God's children, when compared with the children of darkness, should declare without a word that God is good,"[320] insinuating that a Christian's witness to the unsaved around them will depend on their outward appearance.

Christian author Gwen Shamblin, who wrote *The Weigh Down Diet,* told *The Wall Street Journal* that "Grace does not go down into the pigpen."[321] A former fan of Shamblin's told *The Journal* that Shamblin was implying the physically obese might not make it into heaven.[322] Around the same time *Globe* ran an article about Shamblin titled "Fat People Don't Go To Heaven."[323]

Making matters worse, many Christian authors tend to mistake the biblically ideal body for the culturally ideal body. Griffith wrote:

> Christian literature about fitness, weight-loss, and beauty frequently instructs its readers to uphold a pleasing image in the world, as standard bearers of Jesus' love and prototypes of the redeemed life to which non-Christians hopefully would aspire. Yet it embraces American ideals of slender beauty which stand in glaring contrast to attitudes in the developing world that have long associated fat with beauty, wealth, and merit or divine blessing.[324]

Further bolstering the notion that definitions of beauty are culturally relative, journalist Esther Honig sent an image of herself to nearly forty graphic designers in twenty-five countries such as Sri Lanka, Ukraine, the Philippines, and Kenya. She simply requested the designers use Photoshop to make her look "beautiful."

Honig published the altered photos on her website to demonstrate how varied the concept of beauty is across the world. According to Honig, the images are "intriguing and insightful in their own right; each one is a reflection of both the personal and cultural concepts of beauty that pertain to their creator."[325]

Dark But Lovely

In Song of Solomon, the Shulammite woman makes a staggering assertion:

> I am dark, but lovely, O daughters of Jerusalem, Like the tents of Kedar, Like the curtains of Solomon.[326]

In Jerusalem light skin was a sign of affluence and beauty. The word "dark," in this passage, refers to the tan complexion of those lower in status who were forced to work outside in the sun. (The "tents of Kedar" were made of goat hides that grew dark from exposure to the elements; thus the comparison.) Despite the stigma of her appearance, the woman asserts that she is "dark but lovely."

Like the Shulammite woman, the world needs those who are willing to believe in their beauty, despite the milieu that surrounds them.

Griffith seems to agree, pointing to Neva Coyle as a diamond in the fitness culture's rough. Coyle authored several bestselling Christian diet books, traversed the country giving weight loss seminars, and then gained back 100 of the pounds she had lost.

Coyle eventually came to accept the extra pounds, and concluded that God loved her anyways. After this epiphany she became "angry that I had been so unmerciful and shallow with myself and other large Christians."[327]

Coyle went on to write *Loved on a Grander Scale*, a book to help those who struggle with weight learn to accept themselves as they are. She also produced a workout video for large women, *Fit for a King*. Unfortunately, sales of these resources waned in comparison to her prior work; there's just not much demand for those who teach us how to be "dark but lovely."

Griffith asserts:

> What we do with our bodies, how we work to make them ever appealing and desirable, the health care policies we obtain for ourselves and allow for others—all of these are religious matters. They speak louder than our words about what kinds of bodies we adore and what types we despise or at least are willing to abandon. If no critique emerges to challenge today's Christian fitness and beauty culture, we may soon be faced with a still narrower set of Christian exemplars: an army of born-again bodies and malnourished souls.[328]

All Sizes and Shapes

Most of creation was merely spoken into being, but on the sixth day God bent down and picked up the dust.[329] With the passion of an artist canvassing the portrait of a majestic lion, we were rendered—except God looked at *himself* when he painted us. Unlike the animals, our human bodies were handcrafted by God. The lumps, scars, cellulite, and awkward disproportions of which we are ashamed are all God's handiwork. *Our bumps are his brush strokes.*

The shapes of our bodies may not be perfect, but they are holy. To hold a poor image of one's body, then, is an indictment of *his* goodness, not ours. Likewise, as we learn to accept the goodness of our own embodiment, so also can we more fully embrace the goodness of God.

Huffington Post contributor Zanthe Taylor learned to better esteem her body by spending some time at a Korean spa, where swimsuits are not permitted:

> Perhaps I'm naïve, but I'm stunned—really, genuinely stunned—by the vast variety of women's bodies I see there. There are women of all, and I really do mean all, sizes and shapes. The sheer range of shapes we come in is literally marvelous. I'm also surprised how much is revealed when clothes are stripped away: it's far more intimate than the beach, where even tiny swimsuits disguise and guide the flesh in various aesthetic directions. Also, the requirement that we all be naked removes much of the judgment that accompanies beachside people-watching.[330]

I recently spent a day at a Korean spa located in Fullerton, California, and was moved to see fathers bathing nude with their young sons in a context free of pretense. In this setting children learn, at a young age, how to properly comport and esteem their bodies. Taylor goes on to explain how her daughters benefited from the experience as well:

> I've had several revelations prompted by this astounding array of body types. First, not one woman I've ever seen here looks anything like the women we see in magazines or on screen. Some have good figures, sure, but not one has the flat belly, slim hips and large breasts that you'd imagine are standard equipment from media images. Really: NOT ONE. What a gift for young girls to see real women, and I don't mean the occasional "plus size" (size 8) model who releases a widely publicized nude photo. No one looks much like her, either, for the record. My daughters are too young to understand this yet, but I'm hoping that as they grow older they will know, in a way that goes beyond the abstract, that real women have bumps and lumps, cellulite in places you didn't even know you could have cellulite, scars, tattoos, and funny-shaped breasts and areolas. Skinny girls can have flabby tummies, and fat women can be gorgeous. I would say that nudity is the great equalizer, except it's actually the opposite: nudity reveals how immensely varied we are. And it also demonstrates how grossly manipulated we've been when it comes to seeing our own bodies.[331]

Urban Alienation

In her article "Why We Need to Bring Back the Art of Communal Bathing," Jamie Mackay wrote:

> Living in a society where actual nudity has been eclipsed by idealised or pornographic images of it, many of us are, independently of our will, disgusted by hairy backs, flabby bellies and "strange-looking" nipples. The relatively liberal attitude towards such issues in countries such as Denmark, where nudity in the bathhouse is the norm, and in some cases mandatory, exemplifies how the practice might help renormalise a basic sense of diversity and break through the rigid laws that regulate the so-called "normal body".[332]

Mackay asserts that communal bathing has a meaning that extends far beyond personal hygiene:

> The eclipse of communal bathing is one symptom of a wider global transformation, away from small ritualistic societies to vast urban metropolises populated by loose networks of private individuals. This movement has been accompanied by extraordinary benefits, such as the mass availability and movement of services and commodities, but it has also contributed to rampant loneliness, apathy and the emergence of new psychological phenomena, from depression to panic and social anxiety disorders. "Urban alienation", a term much-used by sociologists at the start of the 20th century, has become a cliché for describing today's world.[333]

Mackay believes the reinvention of bathhouses would "compensate for the erosion of public spaces elsewhere."[334] She wrote:

> This is a simple principle: that being physically present with one another makes us more aware of ourselves, and those around us, as biological—not purely linguistic and intellectual—organisms. The ghostly figures that slide past on trains and buses can, in such a space, cease to appear as abstract ideas or numbers and become human once again . . . Directly experiencing other real bodies, touching and

> smelling them, is also an important way of understanding our own bodies which otherwise must be interpreted through the often distorted, sanitised and Photoshopped mirrors of advertising, film and other media.[335]

An Act of Worship

Indeed, nothing remedies body image issues faster than spending some quality naked time with other imperfect bodies. I have found that even being naked while I'm alone is healing. I don't know why, but whenever I take off my clothes to clean, study, or simply reflect, whatever I'm doing actually gets easier—even prayer. It clears my head and gives me a profound sense of connection and release—as if, by removing my clothes, I am throwing off the last remaining connection to society and its rituals, thus baring my soul to God with nothing in the way.

Kyle Hamilton Barr wrote about his experience visiting a nude resort:

> My plan was to spend the day before the Lord naked and unashamed, so I brought my journal, headphones to listen to worship music, and my Bible . . . I then picked a lawn chair away from others so I could listen to music and not be disturbed as I read and journaled. It was very freeing to be there and I literally felt vulnerable and bare before God. I found it very easy to commune with God on a deep, honest level for the hours that I was there. A new layer of shame concerning my body broke off as I did this that day. The entire experience was actually very peaceful and innocent. In some way, I felt as if I was regaining something of childhood innocence.[336]

There is something about becoming more connected to our physical bodies that makes us more connected to God. When I step out of the shower and take a good long look at my body in the mirror, I remind myself it was crafted in the *very image* of God. Affirming my body brings honor and glory to the one who fashioned it, and turns a post-shower shave into an act of worship.

English historian and novelist Charles Kingsley wrote, "When I feel very near God I always feel such a need to undress."[337]

Hadaka no Tsukiai

On his YouTube Channel *Only in Japan*, John Daub visits a public bath. While neck deep in bubbling water, he asserts, "One thing that really confused me when I came to Japan and went to the Onsen is that Japanese are quite shy when they're talking with strangers, but yet here they can come to an Onsen or Sento and be totally free; not shy at all with their nudity."[338]

For clarity on the subject, Daub turned to his ninety-four-year-old neighbor "Mr. Seiichi," who explained:

> These days many people talk about shyness with nudity but many years ago we didn't have that feeling. But when you're naked with everyone, what can you do, right? Whether you are a rich or poor person, when you're naked, you are [all] the same.[339]

There's a Japanese phrase, *hadaka no tsukiai* (裸の付き合い), which basically means *we're all the same when we're naked*. Mackay wrote:

> Today, many people are turning to yoga, mindfulness and other mind-body practices as a private means of resolving the sense of "disembodiment" that can arise from a cramped life spent in metro carriages and hunched over computer screens. The bathhouse could provide a similar space to focus on the body but, crucially, it would do so at the collective level, bringing corporeality and touch back into the sphere of social interaction. The Japanese call this *hadaka no tsukiai* ("naked association") or, in the words of a new generation, "skinship."[340]

Mackay further illustrates the socially equalizing power of communal bathing:

> It is often forgotten that the Roman baths were a space where people of different social classes would wash side

> by side. Throughout the Empire, the bathhouse played a democratising role in which different races and ages were brought into contact. According to the historian Mary Beard, even the emperor, admittedly protected by bodyguards and a team of slaves, would frequently bathe with the people.[341]

Daub concludes, "Here in Japan, it's normal to share a bath. It's a form of communication. So if a stranger talks to you in the bath, don't freak out. To many, there's no better place to be open; be your true self. It's just part of Japanese culture. When you leave the bath house and go outside, I guess that's when things change, and people return to their rank and file in work and life."[342]

High school football coach Ron Chappell told *The Oregonian* he's noticed a trend among players who cleanse after practice. "The more kids we have shower, the better team we have,"[343] he said, explaining that kids who shower together are more comfortable with one another and have better camaraderie on the field.

When I think about those football players, I wonder if the same concept might apply to society at large. Might learning to better accept our bodies make us *all* play better together? Is it possible that, by loving our bodies more, somehow we'll also be empowered to love each other more?

Christianity Today blogger Amy Julia Becker read Zanthe Taylor's account of visiting a Korean spa with her young daughters and was "struck by how much the experience could help her form—for herself and her daughters—a positive understanding of her body as a good gift rather than a necessary but corrupted vessel."[344]

Becker concludes, "Perhaps the experience of nakedness has something to teach me about the freedom of being accepted, as I am, without needing to cover up my flaws or brokenness. Perhaps nakedness has something to teach me about grace."[345]

Endnotes

1. Clapp, *Tortured Wonders*, 25–26.
2. West, *Theology of the Body*, 3.
3. 1 Cor 6:19 NKJV.
4. 2 Cor 5:6–8.
5. Rom 7:24 NKJV.
6. Gal 5:16–17.
7. Berry, *The Unauthorized Guide*, 72.
8. Wiseman, "The Body," 3–4.
9. Plato, *Phaedo*, 66b–67a.
10. Matt 19:12 NASB.
11. Berry, *The Unauthorized Guide*, 81.
12. Berry, *The Unauthorized Guide*, 81.
13. Berry, *The Unauthorized Guide*, 82.
14. Augustine, *Confessions*, [XVII] 23, 138.
15. Winner, *Real Sex*, 33.
16. Berry, *The Unauthorized Guide*, 15.
17. Clapp, *Tortured Wonders*, 18.
18. West, *Theology of The Body*, 6.
19. Rom 1:20 NKJV.
20. Theology of The Body, Pope John Paul II, February 20, 1980.

21. Rana, *The Cell's Design*, 23.
22. Mandino, *The Greatest Miracle*, 95.
23. Simmons, *What Darwin*, 33–34.
24. Lewis, *The Problem*, 34.
25. Rana, *The Cell's Design*, 71.
26. Ryan, "The Body Language," 72–73.
27. Newell, *Echo*, 83–84.
28. Renoe, "The Naked Jesus."
29. Hatton, "Teaching God's Design for Breasts."
30. Stone, *Names of God*, sec. Derivation and Meaning of the Name, para. 5.
31. Stone, *Names of God*, sec. Derivation and Meaning of the Name, para. 6.
32. Isa 60:15–16 NKJV.
33. Isa 66:11–13 NKJV.
34. 1 Pet 2:2–3 NKJV.
35. Berry, *The Unauthorized Guide*, 58–59.
36. Eph 6:12 NKJV (emphasis mine).
37. Clapp, *Tortured Wonders*, 39.
38. Matt 5:27–28 NKJV.
39. West, *Theology of the Body*, 28.
40. Berry, *The Unauthorized Guide*, 19.
41. Berry, *The Unauthorized Guide*, 58.
42. Ryan, "The Body Language," 73–74.
43. West, *Theology of the Body*, 27.
44. West, *Theology of the Body*, 29.
45. West, *Theology of the Body*, 10.

46. Eph 5:28–32 NKJV.

47. West, *Theology of the Body*, 2.

48. Bell, *Sex God*, 43.

49. West, *Theology of the Body*, 33.

50. Bell, *Sex God*, 50.

51. Gaga, "Born This Way."

52. 1 Cor 6:13–15a NKJV.

53. Eph 5:30 NKJV (emphasis mine).

54. Luke 24:51.

55. John 14:26.

56. Rolheiser, *The Holy Longing*, 79.

57. The prayer "Christ Has No Body Now But Yours," though widely attributed to St. Teresa, is not found in her writings. I am taking this quote to mean Christ has no body but ours on *earth*, as Christ does exist bodily in heaven.

58. 2 Cor 3:3 NKJV.

59. 2 Cor 4:7 NKJV.

60. Iacoboni, Woods, Brass, Bekkering, Mazziotta, and Rizzolatti, "Cortical Mechanisms."

61. Timmerman wrote, "I wonder if a same-sex desire really isn't a longing for a dopamine high, but a need for a build up of oxytocin in one's body. This is the chemical that is released in droves in a mother when she gives birth. It is the nurture and comfort response in our body and gives us a sense of place and belonging. It is said to reduce fear, and it makes us more generous and empathetic to others. Increases in this chemical are said to come from receiving care from others—touch, holding and the like. For men with one another, it is the love of a father or brother, and I believe the kind love which may not be the orgasmic high of sex, but is what men who struggle

with sexualizing their same-sex needs long for." Timmerman, *A Bigger World*, 33.

62. *Agapē*, which means love, i.e., affection or benevolence.

63. Ryan, "Toward a Positive," 46.

64. Gen 3:7ab NKJV.

65. Wright, *Shame Off You*, 66.

66. Gen 3:10.

67. Gen 3:7c–8 NKJV.

68. The first visual depiction of the bathing machine appeared in John Settrington's panoramic view of Scarborough in 1735, but an early form of this vehicle was referenced by the diarist Nicholas Blundell in 1721. Ferry, *Beach Huts*, 6.

69. Eggen, "Sculpted Bodies," June 25, 2005.

70. John 20:6–7; Luke 23:34; Mark 15:24; Matt 27:35; John 19:23. In the latter reference, the post-Victorian NIV makes a special point of telling the reader that the guards who took Jesus' clothes left "the undergarment remaining," but the more accurate KJV contains no such qualifier.

71. McGee, "An X-Ray," para. 59.

72. Renoe, "The Naked Jesus." It is in this same vein that Jesus is almost invariably shown exiting the tomb fully clothed, despite Scripture's clear assertion to the contrary (John 20:6–7).

73. Personal correspondence.

74. A team of scientists in Germany has used lice to try and date the invention of clothing. Head lice live solely on the human scalp, while body lice inhabit only those areas covered by clothing. Dr. Mark Stoneking, from the Max Planck Institute for Evolutionary Anthropology in Leipzig, used DNA sequencing to estimate the origin of body lice, and thus the possible origin of human clothing. His study dated the invention of clothing to around 70,000 BC, with a 40,000-year margin

of error. This data conflicts with the beliefs of many Christian scientists, who date the creation of the earth to approximately 6,000 years ago. Kittler, Kayser, and Stoneking, "Molecular Evolution."

75. Evidence of Greek nudity in sport comes from the numerous surviving depictions of athletes: sculptures, mosaics and vase paintings.

76. Delaney, *The Celts*, 31.

77. Owen, "Shower Together," para. 3.

78. Johnson, "Students Still Sweat," para. 5.

79. Johnson, "Students Still Sweat," para. 23.

80. Johnson, "Students Still Sweat," para. 25.

81. Johnson, "Students Still Sweat," para. 27.

82. Johnson, "Students Still Sweat," para. 9.

83. Johnson, "Students Still Sweat," para. 30.

84. Johnson, "Students Still Sweat," para. 28.

85. Johnson, "Students Still Sweat," para. 8.

86. Johnson, "Students Still Sweat," para. 14.

87. Senelick, "Men, Manliness," para. 4.

88. Owen, "Shower Together," para. 18.

89. Johnson, "Students Still Sweat," para. 16–17.

90. Sicha, "Men's Locker Room," para. 4.

91. Sicha, "Men's Locker Room," para. 5.

92. Stern, "If You Are Not Comfortable," para. 1.

93. Fleming, "Nothing to See," para. 3.

94. Scott, "The 12 Worst Guys," para. 6.

95. Beck, "The Private Lives," para. 10.

96. Beck, "The Private Lives," para. 28–29.
97. Beck, "The Private Lives," para. 29.
98. Beck, "The Private Lives," para. 29.
99. Lowder, "Homophobia," para. 3.
100. Middlemist, Knowles, and Matter, "Personal Space."
101. Beck, "The Private Lives," para. 51.
102. Beck, "The Private Lives," para. 52.
103. Beck, "The Private Lives," para. 10.
104. Scott, "The 12 Worst Guys," bullet 7.
105. Scott, "The 12 Worst Guys," bullet 6.
106. Scott, "The 12 Worst Guys," bullet 3.
107. Scott, "The 12 Worst Guys," bullet 2.
108. Gen 3:11 NKJV.
109. Theology of The Body, Pope John Paul II, December 12, 1979.
110. Bradshaw, *Healing the Shame*, 80–81.
111. Mead, "Taking the Role."
112. Bradshaw, *Healing the Shame*, 66.
113. Bradshaw, *Healing the Shame*, 81.
114. Bradshaw, *Healing the Shame*, 80.
115. Gaddis, "What Happens," para. 1.
116. Gaddis, "What Happens," para. 13.
117. Gaddis, What Happens," para. 28.
118. Schwyzer, "The Male Body," para. 1.
119. Schwyzer, "The Male Body," para. 1.
120. Schwyzer, "The Male Body," para. 3.
121. Schwyzer, "The Male Body," para. 6.

122. Gaddis, "What Happens," para. 15.
123. Coffey, "Baby Boy Doll," para. 3.
124. Beyer, "Why I'd Rather," para. 3.
125. Beyer, "Why I'd Rather," para. 6–7.
126. Beyer, "Why I'd Rather," para. 4.
127. Coffey, "Baby Boy Doll," para. 9.
128. Beyer, "Proper or Made-Up," para. 3.
129. Beyer, "Proper or Made-Up," para. 6.
130. Beyer, "Proper or Made-Up," para. 7.
131. Beyer, "Proper or Made-Up," para. 8.
132. Szreter and Fisher, *Sex Before*, 273.
133. Szreter and Fisher, *Sex Before*, 275.
134. Szreter and Fisher, *Sex Before*, 276.
135. Masquelier, *Dirt*, 2.
136. Anonymous comment, "How Old," para. 4 (paraphrased).
137. Barr, *The Touch*, 59.
138. Bradshaw, *Healing the Shame*, 80.
139. Moriss-Roberts, "Cockocracy," para. 7.
140. Diamond, *Why Is Sex*, 145.
141. Savage, in Spitz, *Unhung Hero*.
142. Bordo, *The Male Body*, 70.
143. Bordo, *The Male Body*, 71.
144. Moote, in Spitz, *Unhung Hero*.
145. Bordo, *The Male Body*, 104.
146. Bordo, *The Male Body*, 94–95.
147. West, *Theology of the Body*, 26–27.

148. Padilla, "Transparency," para. 13.

149. Padilla, Campos, Tanquary, and Beckwith, "Physical Transparency."

150. Padilla, Campos, Tanquary, and Beckwith, "Physical Transparency."

151. Padilla, Campos, Tanquary, and Beckwith, "Physical Transparency."

152. Padilla, Campos, Tanquary, and Beckwith, "Physical Transparency."

153. Benjamin, "Naked and Unafraid," para. 11–12.

154. Timmerman, *A Bigger World*, chap. 8, 35.

155. Padilla, Campos, Tanquary, and Beckwith, "Physical Transparency."

156. Padilla, Campos, Tanquary, and Beckwith, "Physical Transparency."

157. Padilla, Campos, Tanquary, and Beckwith, "Physical Transparency."

158. Padilla, Campos, Tanquary, and Beckwith, "Physical Transparency."

159. Padilla, Campos, Tanquary, and Beckwith, "Physical Transparency."

160. Fleming, "Nothing to See," para. 22.

161. Helgeland, *42*.

162. Helgeland, *42* (film).

163. Fleming, "Nothing to See," para. 16.

164. Fleming, "Nothing to See," para. 1.

165. Fleming, "Nothing to See," para. 14.

166. Fleming, "Nothing to See," para. 14.

167. "Question," para. 1–2.

168. Friedman, *A Mind of Its Own*, 39.

169. Friedman, *A Mind of Its Own*, 18.

170. Friedman, *A Mind of Its Own*, 25.

171. Bordo, *The Male Body*, 45.

172. Bordo, *The Male Body*, 55.

173. Bordo, *The Male Body*, 59.

174. *The Oxford Dictionary*.

175. Bordo, *The Male Body*, 98.

176. West, *Theology of the Body*, 28.

177. According to a survey conducted by the Barna Group in the US. In 2014, 64 percent of self-identified Christian men and 15 percent of self-identified Christian women view pornography at least once a month (compared to 65 percent of non-Christian men and 30 percent of non-Christian women). Barna Group, 2014 Pornography Survey and Statistics.

178. "Shame on You," para. 4.

179. "Shame on You," para. 3.

180. Hatton, *Meeting at the River*, 67.

181. Hatton, *Meeting at the River*, 86.

182. Hatton, *Meeting at the River*, 157.

183. Hatton, *Meeting at the River*, 52.

184. Hatton, *Meeting at the River*, 172.

185. Hatton, *Meeting at the River*, 52.

186. Hatton, *Meeting at the River*, 64.

187. Timmerman, *A Bigger World*, chap. 8, 41.

188. "How to Quit," para. 7.

189. Landau, "Men See," para. 1.

190. Reist, "Growing Up," para. 8.

191. Reist, "Growing Up," para. 14.

192. Reist, "Growing Up," para. 11.

193. Lewis, *Mere Christianity*, 96.

194. Clapp, *Tortured Wonders*, 66–67.

195. Hatton, *Meeting at the River*, 166.

196. "Penis Size," para. 1.

197. Keuls, *The Reign*, 68.

198. Fleming, "Nothing to See," para. 6.

199. LeValley, "Ancient India," vol. 6.4.

200. Complete nudity among men and complete or near-complete nudity among women is still common for Mursi, Surma, Nuba, Karimojong, Kirdi, Dinka, and sometimes Maasai people in Africa, as well as Matses, Yanomami, Suruwaha, Xingu, Matis and Galdu people in South America. Tokarev, "What If Nudity."

201. Mackay, "Why We Need," para. 1.

202. Frost, *Christian Body*, Kindle locations 147–49.

203. Frost, *Christian Body*, Kindle locations 150–58.

204. Stone, "Immodesty," para. 1,3.

205. Stone, "Immodesty," para. 2.

206. Frost, *Christian Body*, Kindle locations 301–3.

207. Frost, *Christian Body*, Kindle locations 157–58.

208. Hatton, *Meeting at the River*, 77.

209. Frost, *Christian Body*, Kindle locations 490–94.

210. Stone, "Immodesty," para. 5.

211. Evans, "Modesty," para. 15.

212. Boyle, "Hero Teen," para. 3.

213. Boyle, "Hero Teen," para. 11.

214. Heinlein, *Stranger*, 135–36.

215. Tucker, *From Jerusalem*, 206.

216. Labaca, "All Things to All Men,", 245.

217. 1 Cor 9:12d NKJV.

218. Labaca, "All Things to All Men,", 245.

219. Hatton, *Meeting at the River*, 126.

220. Pulley, "Five American," para. 2.

221. Pulley, "Five American," para. 2.

222. Pulley, "Five American," para. 3.

223. Mora, "Game of Thrones," para. 18–19.

224. Liffman, "The Best Countries," para. 8.

225. "Male Physical," para. 4.

226. Dunn, "Four Lies," para. 5.

227. McAllister, "How To Stop," para. 39.

228. McAllister, "How To Stop," para. 9.

229. McAllister, "How To Stop," para. 16–17.

230. Timmerman, *A Bigger World*, chap. 6, 51.

231. Pulley, "Five American," para. 5.

232. Frost, *Christian Body*, Kindle locations 138–43.

233. Frost, *Christian Body*, Kindle locations 127–29.

234. Frost, *Christian Body*, Kindle locations 140–42.

235. Ruth 3:3, John 21:7, Luke 17:7–8, John 19:23.

236. Frost, *Christian Body*, Kindle locations 398–400, 403–6.

237. Lev 20:17 NKJV.

238. Lev 20:19–21 NKJV.

239. Lev 20:18 NKJV.

240. Gen 9:22 NKJV.

241. Gen 9:24 NKJV.

242. Gen 9:23cde NKJV.

243. Ezek 16:8cdef NIV.

244. Frost, *Christian Body*, Kindle locations 170–71.

245. David Hatton, personal correspondence, June 2, 2016.

246. Hatton, *Meeting at the River*, 159.

247. 1 Tim 2:9bcd–10 NKJV.

248. Evans, “Modesty,” para. 9.

249. Frost, *Christian Body*, Kindle locations 519–20, 560–62.

250. Henry, *Unabridged Matthew*, Kindle locations 339556–58.

251. Hatton, *Meeting at the River*, 149.

252. Anderson, *Earthen Vessels*, 49.

253. Exod 2:5–7.

254. 2 Sam 12:1-4.

255. Exod 22:25–27 NKJV.

256. Frost, *Christian Body*, Kindle locations 630–31.

257. Luke 3:11 NKJV.

258. Matt 25:36a NKJV.

259. Matt 24:18 NKJV.

260. John 21:7 KJV.

261. John 20:10–16 NKJV (emphasis mine).

262. Redman, “Undignified.”

263. 2 Sam 6:14–16, 20–22 NKJV.

264. Mic 1:8 NKJV.

265. 1 Sam 19:24 NKJV.

266. Gen 2:25.

267. Hatton, *Meeting at the River*, 34.

268. Acts 9:36–41.

269. Matt 21:8 NKJV.

270. Matt 5:40 NKJV.

271. Frost, *Christian Body*, Kindle locations 815–19.

272. John 21:7 KJV.

273. John 21:7 NASB (emphasis mine).

274. Ruth 3:3 NASB (emphasis mine).

275. Luke 17:7–8 NASB (emphasis mine).

276. John 13:3a–5 NKJV.

277. Frost, *Christian Body*, Kindle locations 880–86.

278. Hatton, *Meeting at the River*, 32–33.

279. Hatton, *Meeting at the River*, 33.

280. Hatton, *Meeting at the River*, 22–23.

281. Hatton, *Meeting at the River*, 167–68.

282. Hatton, *Meeting at the River*, 168.

283. Hatton, *Meeting at the River*, 35.

284. Dallas, Facebook page, accessed May 30, 2016.

285. Dallas, Facebook page, accessed May 30, 2016.

286. Rom 14:13c NKJV

287. 1 Cor 8:9–12 NKJV

288. Seibold, "The Tyranny," para. 26.

289. Seibold, "The Tyranny," para. 33.

290. Seibold, "The Tyranny ," para. 19, 36.

291. 1 Thess 5:22 KJV.

292. John 7:24 NKJV.

293. Strong, *The Exhaustive Concordance.*

294. Luke 7:36–38 NKJV.

295. Matt 15:16–20.

296. Augustine, *City of God,* book XII, sec. 8, para. 2.

297. Evans, "Modesty," para. 6.

298. Evans, "Modesty," para. 6.

299. Evans, "Modesty," para. 17.

300. Evans, "Modesty," para. 4-5, 7.

301. Evans, "Modesty," para. 19.

302. Hanique, "Jessica Rey."

303. Hanique, "Jessica Rey." See also https://www.jessicarey.com/products/decent-exposure-book.

304. Lewis, *Perelandra*, 115.

305. Rock, "Voices," 106.

306. Rock, "Voices," 106.

307. Grogan, *Body Image*, 16.

308. In 1920 a conference of the New York Academy of Science was convened to study the new phenomena of eating disorders. Grogan, *Body Image*, 19.

309. Grogan, *Body Image*, 32. Becker, "Television." Williams, Ricciardelli, McCabe, Waqa, and Bavadra, "Body Image."

310. Grogan, *Body Image*, 31. Negrao and Cordas, "Clinical characteristics." Kim and Kim, "Body Weight." Nagami, "Eating Disorders."

311. Bordo, *The Male Body*, 69–70.

312. Grogan, *Body Image*, 9–10.

313. Grogan, *Body Image*, 9.

314. Grogan, *Body Image*, 11.

315. Grogan, *Body Image*, 11. Crandall and Martinez, "Culture."

316. Grogan, *Body Image*, 12.

317. Rhode, "Why Looks," para. 10–11.

318. Rhode, "Why Looks," para. 2.

319. Griffith, "Heavenly Hunger," 65.

320. Ortlund, *Disciplines*, 45.

321. Dugan, "Church Lady," para. 18.

322. "Shortly after her public testimony about losing 100 pounds, Mrs. Sneed, 39, confronted Mrs. Shamblin about her other unorthodox view that salvation isn't achieved through God's grace alone but requires effort and repentance. 'I asked her: "When I was 254 pounds, are you telling me I wasn't a child of God?" She said: "That's right."' Mrs. Shamblin says that, indeed, she believes that people who constantly rebel against God's wishes are not going to be saved. 'Grace does not go down into the pigpen,' she says." Dugan, "Church Lady," para. 17-18.

323. "Fat People," 5.

324. Griffith, "Heavenly Hunger," 67.

325. "This Is What," para. 4.

326. Song 1:5 NKJV.

327. Coyle, *Loved*, 10.

328. Griffith, "Heavenly Hunger," 70-71.

329. Psalm 119:73.

330. Taylor, "The Glories," para. 4.

331. Taylor, "The Glories," para. 5.

332. Mackay, "Why We Need," para. 9.

333. Mackay, "Why We Need," para. 3.

334. Mackay, "Why We Need," para. 10.

335. Mackay, "Why We Need," para. 7–8.

336. Barr, *The Touch*, 60–61.

337. Ableman, *Anatomy*, 39.

338. Only in Japan, "Japanese Public."

339. Only in Japan, "Japanese Public."

340. Mackay, "Why We Need," para. 6.

341. Mackay, "Why We Need," para. 8.

342. Only in Japan, "Japanese Public."

343. Owen, "Shower Together," para. 38.

344. Becker, "Kids," para. 8.

345. Becker, "Kids," para. 10.

Bibliography

Ableman, Paul. *Anatomy of Nakedness*. London: Orbis, 1982.

Anderson, Matthew Lee. *Earthen Vessels: Why Our Bodies Matter to Our Faith.* Minneapolis: Bethany House, 2011.

Augustine. *The City of God*. London: Penguin, 2003.

———. *The Confessions of St. Augustine*. London: Dent & Sons, 1920.

Barr, Kyle Hamilton. *The Touch That Transforms: A Personal Journey of Faith, Sexuality, and Healing.* Meadville, PA: Christian Faith, 2018.

Beck, Julie. "The Private Lives of Public Bathrooms." *The Atlantic* (April 16, 2014). http://www.theatlantic.com/health/archive/2014/04/the-private-lives-of-public-bathrooms/360497/.

Becker, Amy Julia. "Kids—Naked and Unashamed." Thin Places. http://www.christianitytoday.com/amyjuliabecker/2014/june/kids-naked-and-unashamed.html.

Becker, A. "Television, Disordered Eating, and Young Women in Fiji: Negotiating Body Image and Identity During Rapid Social Change." *Culture Medicine and Psychiatry* (2004) 28 (4) 533–59.

Bell, Rob. *Sex God: Exploring the Endless Connections between Sexuality and Spirituality*. Grand Rapids: Zondervan, 2007.

Benjamin, A. J. "Naked and Unafraid." The Silent Knight. http://www.thesilentknight.net/blog/naked-and-unafraid.

Berry, Carmen Renee. *The Unauthorized Guide to Sex and the Church*. Nashville: W Publishing Group, 2005.

Beyer, Monica. "Why I'd Rather Explain a Doll Penis Than a Doll with No Genitals." She Knows. http://www.sheknows.com/parenting/articles/1045253/why-a-doll-with-a-penis-isnt-a-big-deal?adbsc=social_20140728_28633726.

———. "Proper or Made-Up Names For Genitals?" She Knows. http://www.sheknows.com/parenting/articles/967843/proper-or-made-up-names-for-genitals.

Bordo, Susan. *The Male Body: A New Look at Men in Public and in Private*. New York: Farrar, Straus and Giroux, 2015.

Boyle, Darren. "Hero Teen Starbucks Barista Gives Breast Feeding Mother Free Coffee After Middle-Aged Woman Branded Her 'Disgusting.'" Dailymail.com. http://www.dailymail.co.uk/news/article-2679041/Hero-teen-Star

bucks-barista-gives-breast-feeding-mother-free-coffee-middle-aged-woman-branded-disgusting.html?ito=social-facebook.

Bradshaw, John. *Healing the Shame That Binds You*. Deerfield Beach, FL: Health Communications, 2005.

Clapp, Rodney. *Tortured Wonders: Christian Spirituality for People, Not Angels*. Grand Rapids: Brazos, 2006.

Coffey, Laura T. "Baby Boy Doll with Realistic-Looking Penis Shocks Some Parents." Today. http://www.today.com/parents/doll-penis-shocks-some-parents-1D80005572.

Coyle, Neva. *Loved on a Grander Scale: Affirmation, Acceptance, and Hope for Women Who Struggle with Their Weight*. Ann Arbor, MI: Servant, 1998.

Crandall, C. S., and R. Martinez. "Culture, Ideology, and Anti-Fat Attitudes." *Personality and Social Psychology Bulletin* (1996) 22, 1165–76.

Daley, Leo Charles. *The Works of St. Augustine*. New York: Monarch, 1965.

Dallas, Joe. Personal Facebook page, accessed May 30, 2016, https://www.facebook.com/joe.dallas.92/posts/10154339806935039?comment_id=10154340836295039¬if_t=like¬if_id=1464842910391776.

Delaney, Frank. *The Celts*. Boston: Little, Brown, 1986.

Diamond, Jared M. *Why Is Sex Fun?* New York: Basic, 1998.

Dugan, Ianthe Jeanne. "Church Lady of Diet Weighs In on Trinity and Her Flock Flees." *Wall Street Journal* (October 30, 2000). https://www.wsj.com/articles/SB972863852671088281?ns=prod/accounts-wsj.

Dunn, Lily. "Four Lies the Church Taught Me About Sex." *Relevant Magazine* (June 10, 2014). http://www.relevantmagazine.com/life/relationships/4-lies-church-taught-me-about-sex.

Eggen, Dan. "Sculpted Bodies And a Strip Act At Justice Dept." *Washington Post*, June 25, 2005. http://www.washingtonpost.com/wp-dyn/content/article/2005/06/24/AR2005062401797.html.

Evans, Rachel Held. "Modesty: I Don't Think it Means What You Think it Means." Qideas.org. http://qideas.org/articles/modesty-i-dont-think-it-means-what-you-think-it-means/.

"Fat People Don't Go To Heaven." *Globe* (November 21, 2000).

Ferry, Kathryn. *Beach Huts and Bathing Machines*. Buckinghamshire: Shire, 2012.

Fleming, David. "Nothing to See Here: A History of Showers in Sports." *ESPN The Magazine* (July 8, 2014). http://www.espn.com/espn/feature/story/_/id/11169006/nfl-showers-hostile-environment-michael-sam-espn-magazine.

Friedman, David M. *A Mind of Its Own: A Cultural History of the Penis*. London: Free Press, 2002.

Frost, Aaron. *Christian Body: Modesty and the Bible*. Kindle ed. N.p.: Aaron Frost, 2018.

Gaddis, Jayson. "What Happens When We Don't Teach Boys about Sex." Jaysongaddis.com. http://www.jaysongaddis.com/what-happens-when-we-dont-teach-boys-about-sex/.

Gaga, Lady. "Born This Way." In *Born This Way*. Lady Gaga. Interscope, 2011, CD.

Griffith, R. Marie. "Heavenly Hunger." Center for Christian Ethics at Baylor University. https://www.baylor.edu/ifl/christianreflection/foodandhunger articlegriffith.pdf.

Grogan, Sarah. *Body Image: Understanding Body Dissatisfaction in Men, Women, and Children*. London: Routledge, 2008.

Hanique, Guillaume. "Jessica Rey - The evolution of the swim suit." YouTube, 9:30. Posted June 17, 2013. https://www.youtube.com/watch?v=WJVHRJbgLz8.

Hatton, David. *Meeting at the River*. N.p.: David Hatton (Printed by CreateSpace), 2013.

———. "Teaching God's Design for Breasts." http://www.pastordavidrn.com/files/Breasts.html.

Helgeland, Brian, director. *42*. United States: Warner Brothers, 2013. DVD.

Heinlein, Robert A. *Stranger in a Strange Land: The Original Uncut Edition*. New York: Ace, 1991.

Henry, Matthew. *Unabridged Matthew Henry's Commentary on the Whole Bible*. Kindle ed. N.p.: OSNOVA, 2010.

"How Old is Too Old For Your Kids to See You Naked?" Savvydaddy.com. http://www.savvydaddy.com/content/age/infant/00324/how-old-too-old-your-kids-see-you-naked.

"How to Quit Porn: 6 Essential Steps." Covenant Eyes. http://www.covenanteyes.com/2012/04/23/how-to-quit-porn-6-essential-steps/ 6-16-2016.

Iacoboni, Marco, Roger P. Woods, Marcel Brass, Harold Bekkering, John C. Mazziotta, and Giacomo Rizzolatti. "Cortical Mechanisms of Human Imitation". *Science* (1999) 286 (5449) 2526–2528. doi:10.1126/science.286.5449.2526. PMID 10617472.

Johnson, Dirk. "Students Still Sweat, They Just Don't Shower." *The New York Times* (April 22, 1996). http://www.nytimes.com/1996/04/22/us/students-still-sweat-they-just-don-t-shower.html.

Keuls, Eva C. *The Reign of the Phallus: Sexual Politics in Ancient Athens*. Berkeley, CA: University of California Press, 1993.

Kim, O., and K. Kim. "Body Weight, Self-Esteem, and Depression in Korean Female Adolescents." *Adolescence* (2001) 36, 315–22.

Kittler, R., M. Kayser, and M. Stoneking. "Molecular Evolution of Pediculus Humanus and the Origin of Clothing". *Current Biology* (2003) 13 (16) 1414–17. doi:10.1016/S0960-9822(03)00507-4. PMID 12932325.

Labaca, Alejandro. "All Things to All Men." In *Nudity & Christianity*, edited by Jim C. Cunningham, 245. Bloomington, IN: AuthorHouse, 2006.

Landau, Elizabeth. "Men See Bikini-Clad Women as Objects, Psychologists Say." CNN.com. http://www.cnn.com/2009/HEALTH/02/19/women.bikinis.objects/index.html?eref=rss_us.

LeValley, Paul. "Ancient India," Clothed with the Sun, Vol. 6.4. Oshkosh, WI: The Naturists, Inc., Winter, 1986–87.

Lewis, C. S. *Mere Christianity*. London: Collins, 1955.

———. *Perelandra*. New York: Scribner, 1996.

———. *The Problem of Pain*. London: HarperCollins, 2002.

Liffman, Taz. "The Best Countries for Heterosexual Men to Hold Hands (in Case You Were Wondering)." Geckosadventures.com. http://www.geckos adventures.com/tales/best-countries-men-hold-hands-case-wondering/.

Lowder, J. Bryan. "Homophobia in the Bathroom." Outward. http://www.slate.com/blogs/outward/2014/04/16/public_bathrooms_and_homophobia_why_are_men_afraid_to_pee_together.html.

Mackay, Jamie. "Why We Need to Bring Back the Art of Communal Bathing." Aeon. https://aeon.co/ideas/why-we-need-to-bring-back-the-art-of-com munal-bathing.

"Male Physical Intimacy." Free Northerner. http://freenortherner.com/2015 /10/23/male-physical-intimacy/.

Mandino, Og. *The Greatest Miracle in the World*. New York: Bantam, 1997.

Masquelier, Adeline Marie. "Introduction." In *Dirt, Undress, and Difference: Critical Perspectives on the Body's Surface*, edited by Adeline Masquelier, 1–33. Bloomington, IN: Indiana University Press, 2006.

McAllister, D. C. "How To Stop Sexualizing Everything." The Federalist, December 28, 2015. http://thefederalist.com/2015/12/28/how-to-stop-sexualizing-everything/.

McGee, J. Vernon. "An X-Ray of the Cross." http://articles.ochristian.com/article15577.shtml.

Mead, George Herbert. "Taking the Role of the Other." eNotes.com. March 4, 2019. https://www.enotes.com/research-starters/george-herbert-mead-taking-role-other.

Middlemist, R. D., E. S. Knowles, and C. F. Matter. "Personal Space Invasions in the Lavatory: Suggestive Evidence for Arousal." *Personality and Social Psychology Bulletin* (1976) 33, 541–46. 10.1037/0022-3514.33.5.541.

Mora, Teresa Larraz. "Game of Thrones' Martin: I Like My Characters to Suffer." Reuters. https://uk.reuters.com/article/uk-books-author-george martin/game-of-thrones-martin-i-like-my-characters-to-suffer-idUKBRE86J15220120720.

Morriss-Roberts, Christopher. "Cockocracy: Size Matters in the Locker Room, Researcher Finds." Outsports. https://www.outsports.com/2014 /3/17/5515302/penis-size-matters-locker-room-gay-straight-study.

Newell, J. Philip. *Echo of the Soul: The Sacredness of the Human Body*. Harrisburg, PA: Morehouse, 2002.

Nagami, Y. "Eating Disorders in Japan: A Review of the Literature." *Psychiatry and Clinical Neuroscience* (1997) 51, 339–46.

Negrao, Andre, and Táki Cordás. "Clinical Characteristics and Course of Anorexia Nervosa in Latin America, a Brazilian Sample." *Psychiatry Research* (1996) 62, 17–21. 10.1016/0165-1781(96)02981-2.

Only in Japan. "Japanese Public Bathing Exposed: The Naked Truth." YouTube. 8:57. Posted January 26, 2015. https://www.youtube.com/watch?v=2rp KDnNLtxU.

Ortlund, Anne. *Disciplines of the Beautiful Woman.* Nashville: W Publishing Group, 1984.

Owen, Wendy. "Shower Together at School? No Way, Dude." The Oregonian Extra (July 22, 2009). http://blog.oregonlive.com/oregonianextra/2009/07/shower_together_at_school_no_w.html.

The Oxford Dictionary. Oxford: Oxford University Press, 1992.

Padilla, Richard. "Transparency: Skinny Dipping, Nakedness, Homosexuality, Identity Crises." The 4T's and the Church. http://www.the4tsandthechurch.com/blogs/2017/1/9/transparency.

Padilla, Richard, Stephen Campos, Stephan Tanquary, and Matt Beckwith. "Physical Transparency: Loving Christians Who Struggle with Homosexuality Through Nudity and the Locker Room." The 4T's and the Church. http://www.the4tsandthechurch.com/4ts-podcast-1/.

"Penis Size in Classical Art." Penis Sizes. http://www.penissizes.org/penis-size-art.

Plato. *Plato's Phaedo.* Oxford: Clarendon, 1911.

Pulley, Anna. "Five American Sex Norms Europeans Probably Think Are Insane." Alternet. http://www.alternet.org/sex-amp-relationships/5-american-sex-norms-europeans-probably-think-are-insane.

"Question: What If I Get An Erection?" The Real Rub. https://therealrub.wordpress.com/2012/02/18/what-if-i-get-an-erection/.

Rana, Fazale. *The Cell's Design: How Chemistry Reveals the Creator's Artistry.* Grand Rapids: Baker, 2008.

Redman, Matt. "Undignified." In *Blessed Be Your Name: The Songs of Matt Redman Volume 1.* Survivor Records, 2005, CD.

Reist, Melinda Tankard. "Growing Up in Pornland: Girls Have Had It with Porn Conditioned Boys." ABC Religion and Ethics. http://www.abc.net.au/religion/articles/2016/03/07/4420147.htm.

Renoe, Ethan. "The Naked Jesus." Ethanrenoe.com. https://ethanrenoe.com/2016/04/13/the-naked-jesus/.

Rhode, Deborah L. "Why Looks Are the Last Bastion of Discrimination." *The Washington Post* (May 23, 2010). http://www.washingtonpost.com/wp-dyn/content/article/2010/05/20/AR2010052002298.html.

Rock, Casey. "Voices From the Mat." In *Reclaiming the Body In Christian Spirituality*, edited by Thomas Ryan, 95–115. New York: Paulist, 2004.

Rolheiser, Ronald. *The Holy Longing: the Search for a Christian Spirituality.* New York: Image, 2014.

Ryan, Thomas. "The Body Language of Faith." In *Reclaiming the Body In Christian Spirituality*, edited by Thomas Ryan, 57–94. New York: Paulist, 2004.

———. "Toward a Positive Spirituality of the Body." In *Reclaiming the Body In Christian Spirituality*, edited by Thomas Ryan, 21–56. New York: Paulist, 2004.

Seibold, Loren. "The Tyranny of the Weaker Brother." Ministry International Journal for Pastors (November 2012). https://www.ministrymagazine.org/archive/2012/11/the-tyranny-of-the-weaker-brother.

Senelick, Richard. "Men, Manliness, and Being Naked Around Other Men." *The Atlantic* (February 3, 2014). https://www.theatlantic.com/health/archive/2014/02/men-manliness-and-being-naked-around-other-men/282998/.

Sicha, Choire. "Men's Locker Room Designers Take Pity on Naked Millennials." *The New York Times* (December 3, 2015). http://www.nytimes.com/2015/12/04/fashion/mens-style/mens-locker-room-designers-take-pity-on-naked-millennials.html?hpw&rref=fashion&action=click&pgtype=Homepage&module=well-region®ion=bottom-well&WT.nav=bottom-well&_r=0.

Scott, Kyle. "The 12 Worst Guys You Encounter in the Gym Locker Room, Ranked." Crossing Broad. http://www.crossingbroad.com/2014/08/the-12-worst-guys-you-encounter-in-the-gym-locker-room-ranked.html.

Schwyzer, Hugo. "The Male Body: Repulsive or Beautiful?" The Good Men Project. http://goodmenproject.com/ethics-values/the-male-body-repulsive-or-beautiful/.

"Shame on You! A Conversation with 'A Dirty Shame''s John Waters, Selma Blair, and Johnny Knoxville." AMC.com. https://www.amc.com/talk/2004/09/shame-on-you-a.

Simmons, Geoffrey S. *What Darwin Didn't Know*. Eugene, OR: Harvest House, 2004.

Spitz, Brian, director. *Unhung Hero*. GreenskyFILMS, 2013, DVD.

Stern, Mark Joseph. "If You Are Not Comfortable Being Naked Around Other People, You Are Not an Adult." Outward. http://www.slate.com/blogs/outward/2015/12/03/locker_room_nudity_is_healthy_and_normal_fear_of_it_is_irrational.html.

Stone, Nathan J. *Names of God*. Chicago: Moody, 2010.

Strong, James. *The Exhaustive Concordance of the Bible: Showing Every Word of the Text of the Common English Version of the Canonical Books, and Every Occurrence of Each Word in Regular Order; Together with Dictionaries of the Hebrew and Greek Words of the Original*. McLean, VA: MacDonald, 1900. https://www.blueletterbible.org/lang/lexicon/lexicon.cfm?Strongs=G3799&t=KJV.

Stone, Rachel Marie. "Immodesty All Over the Map." *Christianity Today* (June 2013). http://www.christianitytoday.com/women/2013/june/immodesty-all-over-map.html.

Szreter, Simon, and Kate Fisher. *Sex before the Sexual Revolution: Intimate Life in England 1918–1963*. Cambridge: Cambridge University Press, 2011.

Taylor, Zanthe. "The Glories of Nudity." HuffPost.com. http://www.huffingtonpost.com/zanthe-taylor/the-glories-of-nudity_b_5352398.html.

"This Is What the Same Woman Looks Like Photoshopped in Different Countries." *Time* (June 27, 2014). http://time.com/2934434/this-is-what-the-same-woman-looks-like-photoshopped-in-different-countries/.

Timmerman, Tim. *A Bigger World Yet: Faith, Brotherhood, & Same Sex Needs.* Newberg, OR: Bird Dog, 2012. Kobo eBooks.

Tokarev, Kirill. "What If Nudity Were a Norm?" Active Naturists. https://activenaturists.net/nudity-ok/.

Tucker, Ruth. *From Jerusalem to Irian Jaya: a Biographical History of Christian Missions*. Grand Rapids: Zondervan, 2004.

West, Christopher. *Theology of the Body for Beginners.* West Chester, PA: Ascension, 2004.

Williams, L. K., L. A. Ricciardelli, M. P. McCabe, G. G. Waqa, and K. Bavadra. "Body Image Attitudes and Concerns Among Indigenous Fijian and European Australian Adolescent Girls." *Body Image: An International Journal of Research* (2006) 3, 275–88.

Winner, Lauren F. *Real Sex: The Naked Truth about Chastity.* Grand Rapids: Brazos, 2006.

Wiseman, James. "The Body In Spiritual Practice." In *Reclaiming the Body In Christian Spirituality*, edited by Thomas Ryan, 1–20. New York: Paulist, 2004.

Wright, Alan D. *Shame Off You*. Sisters, OR: Multnomah, 2005.